# World war 1

Interesting Stories and Random Facts from the First World War

*(The History and Legacy of Britain's Covert Activities during Both Conflicts)*

**Juan Tellez**

Published By **Sharon Lohan**

**Juan Tellez**

*World war 1: Interesting Stories and Random Facts from the First World War (The History and Legacy of Britain's Covert Activities during Both Conflicts)*

**ISBN   978-1-9992555-7-2**

Legal & Disclaimer

Table Of Contents

## Chapter 1: The Causes Of World War 1

Hello, and welcome to the start of our take a look at into the early history and reasons of World War 1. Join us as we go to the beyond to see how lifestyles modified into over a hundred years ago. In the ones days, the world changed into like a jigsaw puzzle with many quantities, every having its non-public precise affiliation. The international have become changing and with it came multiplied tension. It has become similar to the inner of a warm oven in which the tension and temperature have become grade by grade growing. Many elements and narratives have been inflicting this constructing up. Now as we delve into the statistics of this international struggle, we'll find out what the ones had been and the way they performed a function within the war.

(Europe map)

Arms race

In the late 19th to early twentieth century, international locations in Europe had built up massive armies with effective defences. It changed into like a competition to appearance that may additionally need to turn out to be the most powerful. Battleships with huge cannons, lethal weapons, and strong infantrymen regarded to be multiplying each day in the war to pop out on top. But as each usa constructed a stronger navy the greater fearful their neighbors have emerge as.

Imagine in case you lived in a neighborhood and all the houses round you stored building higher partitions. You may likely begin to surprise why they are doing that? Are they hiding a few things or are they getting ready for some component? Well that is precisely the manner it felt for the state's competing in competition to every one-of-a-kind.

Suspicion unfolds like a fog as worldwide places competed to construct the mightiest militaries. It have come to be like a giant hurricane turn out to be building, whole with darkish, threatening clouds just looking in advance to thunder to clap.

Conflicts within the Balkans

Now allows hop on our time device and head over to the Balkans place. This vicinity of Europe become lacking numerous facts, no matter the truth that it have become a critical piece of the general puzzle. Serbs, Croats, Bosnians and lots of others have all known as this great vicinity domestic at one time or another. But much like a puzzle wherein quantities do now not frequently healthy together the ones groups of human beings failed to constantly get along so nicely. Rivalries quick fashioned because the tensions a number of the organizations grew like a raging river.

Imagine the place like a big condo building in which all of them lived, but in which everybody had to beautify their hallway in their non-public way. Conflict has become not unusual as various businesses pursued their non-public desires and vintage wounds reopened As time passed the warmth changed into slowly building as lots as a today's diploma. All it desired modified into a small spark to ignite it proper right into a huge hearth that sparks modified into about to are to be had an event that could shake the whole global.

Sarajevo Assassination

Deep in the coronary heart of the Balkans nestled like a jewel in a crown has become a energetic city named Sarajevo. It changed into very just like a hectic market, whole of human beings from all walks of life going approximately their each day lives. On one fateful day, June twenty eighth, 1914 this everyday metropolis should become the volume for a terrific event that would ship shockwaves throughout the globe.

At the centre of this event became the assassination of Archduke Franz Ferdinand, of Austria-Hungary and his partner Sophie, The Duchess of Hohenberg. The Archduke modified into no normal character. He ends up subsequent in line to be the King of the Austrian-Hungarian Empire. Sophie, his accomplice, modified into dearly in his coronary heart and their love story became one which went in the course of the strict guidelines of royalty. The couple took a go to to Sarajevo, however it have emerge as now not a regular royal visit. On the anniversary of a large struggle, they got here to pay their respects and display appreciation to the locals. They checked out it as a chance to make a clean start and spread goodwill all through their empire.

Things have been an extended manner from calm within the Balkans. The shifting of those international locations spherical like a jigsaw puzzle had caused multiplied tensions within the area. Bosnia and Herzegovina had been annexed with the aid of using Austria-Hungary in 1908 and this had brought on great tension. Wait a minute, what does annex recommend? Annex - technique that a rustic takes over a new piece of land and makes it part of their very personal u. S. Its form of like at the equal time as you upload a contemporary piece for your jigsaw puzzle and it turns into part of the larger picture. But proper right here's the important hassle. When a rustic annexes some one of a kind piece of land, it normally has to check some rules and talk to one of kind international places to make certain everyone is ok with it. Just like you'll probable ask your pals if it's far adequate to function your piece to their puzzle? Annexing is like such as a contemporary piece to a country's puzzle, however its miles finished in a way that makes certain everybody is of the identical opinion and it's miles sincere for every person worried.

Now back to the tale! Amongst the constructing anxiety a thriller employer known as the Black Hand modified into long-established. Gavrilo Princip becomes a well-known member of it. During the busy day of June twenty eighth, 1914 in Sarajevo, Princip and his business enterprise noticed a chance to further their purpose. Many inside the vicinity located the royal Archduke's visit as a photograph in their oppression and that they desired to be freed from it. With a coronary heart entire of dedication and a pistol in his hand, Princip stepped forward. He took aim and shot at the Archduke, who stood for a whole system. The Archduke turns out to be killed at the same time as he collapsed. (King & Woolmans, 2013) (Butcher, 2014)

The assassination changed into now not simply an act of violence however it have emerge as a spark that ignited the flames of World War I. Austria-Hungary come to be furious over the assassination and held Serbia accountable. They declared battle on Serbia which activates a series reaction of activities main to a international war. Sareajo which end up as speedy as a town well-known for its life-style and range had now turned out to be the centre of a global converting event from this component onwards the area become plunged into the darkness of struggle and all because of those fateful images fired on that day.

The assassination's outcomes echoed globally, just like the sound of gunfire did through Sarajevo's streets. Serbia changed into held accountable by Austria and Hungary. But Serbia had many allies similar to pals in the neighborhood who came to their rescue. Russia, which changed into a powerful u. S. On the time, felt its duty to defend Serbia. Russia too had its personal set of allies together with France and the United Kingdom. It become like each U. S. A. Was tangled in a spider net of alliances and the threads had been slowly being pulled aside.

Imagine a line of dominoes; if one falls, the others will fall. The first domino falling changed into the assassination of the Archduke. Dominoes then started out to fall one after the other. Russia despatched navy useful useful resource to Serbia. War grows to be declared through manner of Germany in opposition to Russia. The United Kingdom and France joined in to preserve their word and lower back Russia. The dominoes began out to fall and shortly enough World War 1 had begun. Europe rapid has emerge as like a huge thunderstorm. Suddenly, armies from particular countries started out out to face off and combat each one of a kind. One needs to preserve in mind that this emerge as no ordinary warfare. It changed right into a battle on a scale in evaluation to a few factor the arena had ever seen earlier than. Later we can have a check this in lots, loads more detail so stay tuned! This became the start of World War 1, which may additionally regulate the direction of information in techniques no person might also moreover need to have predicted. The term "July crisis" turns out to be coined to give an explanation for the dramatic increase in tension that took place that month of 1914.

That first actual domino falling which modified into the assassination in Sarajevo the diverse developing tension had commenced the chain response of sports plunging the world into the depths of struggle. It turns out to be a cautionary reminder of the manner reputedly small activities can have protracted way accomplishing and devastating results. We

yourselves for each different exciting have to investigate that after we do awful subjects the consequences can be masses greater than that act itself. Because of these activities, the area changed into approximately to plunge into the darkness and chaos of World War 1 A war like in no manner in advance that.

## Chapter 2: The Start

Greetings, returning younger readers! The dramatic sports that led as much as World War 1 are really well known to you. In the remaining economic disaster we found how early moves and alliances finished out. Now we are about to discover what befell next. In this financial ruin, we're going to dig even deeper into the unfolding drama of the war. Prepare exploration in which we'll journey deeper into the coronary heart of World War 1 statistics.

(World War 1. German infantry advancing)

When the struggle started out it modified into like a big curtain growing on a grand play with many countries stepping out onto the region degree now allow us to introduce a number of those key gamers. Without entering into all of the complicated battles (we are able to try this later), permits find out why Austria-

Hungary, the Ottoman Empire, and Germany allied together. Furthermore we're able to provide a purpose for why France, Russia, and the United Kingdom allied themselves in the direction of them.

At the begin of the twentieth century, large nations like Austria-Hungary, Germany and the Ottoman Empire all desired extra land and strength. Imagine in case you in reality favored automobiles and you preferred to have masses and hundreds of them. Even in case you already had quite a few! Well the ones international locations began out annexing territory from others without asking. Similar to taking cars from every exclusive Some of those international locations had been friends with every one-of-a-kind and on the same time as one among them had been given right into a fight with some different u . S ., their pals favored to help them out. It's a piece like if one in every of your pals had a problem with someone. You might stand with the aid of your friend's element to aid them. Austria-Hungary, Germany and the Ottoman Empire had comparable dreams and joined together to become known as "The Central Powers". But all this amassing of land and assisting pals caused vital issues. Eventually as we discovered in advance this anxiety combined with sports inclusive of the assassination exploded right into a massive, sad occasion known as World War 1.

Now at the alternative component of The Central Powers, there have been 3 unique friends France, Russia and the UK. They failed to like how the ones grasping international locations were taking matters from others due to the reality they believed in something referred to as democracy. This way that people should have a say in how their global places are run and that everybody must be dealt with pretty. Together they decided to upward push as lots because the grasping worldwide places, who have been like bullies in a manner. Ultimately they preferred to stop them from taking more land and inflicting trouble. Thus they joined forces and feature turn out to be known as the Allies. The Central Powers had been the "enemy" that France, Russia, and the UK determined to unite in competition to in World War 1. Germany, Austria-Hungary, the Ottoman Empire and Bulgaria have been all individuals of this business enterprise of Central Powers.

Asia and the Pacific Theatre in World War I

Beyond Europe, the effect of World War 1 changed into felt spherical the area. The waves of warfare may be felt all of the manner at some point of Asia and to the Pacific. The German Empire managed many Pacific colonies, at the side of Papua

New Guinea and Samoa. However, the Allied forces need to expect their friends in Australia and New Zealand for aid there. By taking manage of those close by areas, they was hoping to increase their impact. The Pacific area erupted in violence. Australia invaded Papua Guinea, and New Zealand occupied Nazi-occupied Samoa.

(Imperial Palace grounds in Tokyo, Japan)

Japan, each different Asian USA of the United States, also decided to sign up for the worldwide warfare. In the start, they attacked Germany. Japan observed the warfare as a possibility to seize German-managed territories within the Pacific. In particular, Japan aimed to advantage control of German-controlled territories in China's Shandong Peninsula and the Pacific islands of Micronesia. They set their points of interest on annexing various islands and territories in the Pacific. They moreover planned to capture manipulate of what the Chinese call "Treaty ports." But there has been a deliver from Austria-Hungary referred to as SMS Kaiser in Elisabeth in such a places, called Tsingtao. Japan asked nicely for the supply to go away, however Austria-Hungary said no. Japan was given indignant and declared battle on Austria-Hungary too. They even attacked the supply with their plane. (Fen by, 2014)

In only some months, Japan and its friends within the Allies controlled to take control of all of the locations that belonged to Germany in the Pacific. They left only a few ships which have been inflicting trouble and a few folks that did no longer want to give up in New Guinea. It turned into like a huge workout of seize the flag, however with international locations and territories alternatively!

The African Theatre of World War I

Many African global locations have been moreover concerned in World War 1. Imagine the area as a huge chessboard with exceptional countries shifting their portions. Africa completed an vital function in this chessboard. Germany had colonies in Africa and the Allies favored to seize them. The first battles occurred in East Africa wherein German General Paul von Lettow-Vorbeck led a daring advertising advertising campaign. It became sort of like a excessive-stakes exercise of disguise and are searching out with the German famous using cunning techniques to outsmart his opponents. (Gaudi, 2017)

Indian Support for the Allies

As a growing state, India had a prime effect on World War 1. At the time, India became a colony of the United Kingdom. Essentially this meant they had been under the UK's rule. Back then it changed into a big empire. Indian troops fought on each the European and the Middle Eastern fronts. Valiantly they fought at the thing of the Allies and made important contributions to their cause as they smashed within the course of battlefields like a mythological elephant.

The contributions of Indian troops in World War 1 no longer fine tested their feature as valiant warriors however moreover paved the manner for later political changes in India. The reputation in their sacrifices accomplished a trouble of their war for independence. To nowadays the legacy of brave Indian infantrymen remains remembered and honored.

World War 1 has emerged as fatly progressing and the sector watched on as international places splendor clashed on multiple fronts. But highly-priced time website online visitors as we adventure thru this epic tale we are about to stand some harsh realities. As the struggle advanced it'd quick plunge into a new tough financial disaster a financial ruin full of mud, trenches and tough times. Brace yourselves as our subsequent journey will take us deep into the trenches wherein we are going to find out the cruel and constant nature of trench struggle.

### Chapter 3: Life In The Trenches

Welcome lower returned time fearless time traffic! In the remaining monetary destroy we noticed how the conflict changed into advancing because the arena turned into enthusiastic about clashes on more than one fronts. In this new economic catastrophe it's time to stand a harsh truth. As the war become evolving it emerge as thrust into a brand new technology blanketed with trenches and mainly difficult instances. In this financial ruin we're going to enter into the trenches in which you may discover the gritty and harsh nature of trench war. So prepare yourselves for a difficult adventure that lies earlier.

Imagine your favored pair of footwear. The ones you want to place on for adventures with buddies or for while you play sports activities activities. Now remember the ones shoes were blanketed in thick, gooey dirt that sticks with each step. That modified into only a small pattern of what it turn out to be really like for soldiers at the front traces. Throughout the battlefields, trenches dug into the dirt acted because the "arteries." But the ones tunnel networks have been a bargain more than really trenches; they were an underground worldwide wherein squad dies lived and died. Brave soldiers would likely spend weeks and frequently months within the ones restrained areas in which they have been confronted with isolation, boredom and the fear of unexpected lack of life. Their stories are a testimony to the spirit and power of human beings.

Trench life has become a every day war for survival. Not best did soldiers face the threat of enemy assaults however they had been moreover exposed to intense elements, illnesses and the regular mental strain of combat. The muddy, cold and moist situations ought to regularly turn out to be flooded and infested with rats. When it rained, it become even greater difficult to transport spherical Imagine looking for to pass a in no way-finishing puddle and there's no manner of escaping it. For days on surrender the rain would pour down relentlessly turning the trenches into rivers of mud. Soldiers couldn't surely circulate interior to dry off or heat up. There has become nowhere to live however the trenches, in order that they needed to endure the ones bloodless moist situations with mud squelching beneath their ft.

There became no connoisseur cooking taking location within the trenches both. Biscuits, canned meat and watery soups had been on the each day menu. The canned meat has come to be hard and gritty and the biscuits had been like rock tough crackers. Such food was a much cry from the tasty meals that we now enjoy at domestic with our families. But irrespective of the lack of tasty meals the courageous squad dies made the fantastic of what that they had. Like brothers in a own family they shared their meals and did their brilliant. It turn out to be a lesson that even inside the most difficult of conditions we can also turn out to be loads more difficult than we consider while we art work together.

In the trenches the squad dies had to be on everyday alert to enemy assaults. Explosions and gunfire constantly rang round them making it hard to find a 2nd of peace. Furthermore, they faced harsh weather situations from heavy rains, to freezing winters, to the sweltering warm temperature of summer time. Despite the ones demanding situations they showed extremely good strength, brotherhood and resolution. Together they have become like a group of superheroes helping every different through the tough instances. Unbreakable bonds have been original and they stood with the useful resource of the use of every other to protect their international locations with honour and bravado.

In a manner trench existence changed right into a in no way-completing journey. But it wasn't the regular adventure packed with a laugh but instead it has become full of trouble and sacrifice. Many of the squad dies in the trenches had been more youthful men a long manner away from home surrounded by sudden faces in distant places lands. They missed their family, buddies and the comforts of domestic. Back within the ones days they did not have Wi-Fi, messenger or e mail. So how did they live in touch with loved ones lower again at home?

During World War 1 letters have been written that related squad dies to their loved ones. Soldiers wrote heartfelt letters to their families to percentage their critiques, their hopes and their fears. In the muddy trenches they may write via way of the dim mild of a lantern slight. They may write home to their cherished ones approximately how an awful lot they left out them and the difficulties they were dealing with. Every letter was like sending a bit of them internationally. Families sent their very own letters in go back to the squad dies presenting energy and love to them. These letters had been more than genuinely terms on paper. They have been the lifeblood of family relationships and a fuel for preference in decided instances. Those letters characteristic a reminder that during spite of the horrors of warfare, human connection, compassion, and facts could make us stronger than ever Soldiers moreover wrote down their thoughts and emotions in journals. Many of the details we understand about lifestyles in the trenches come from these diaries. The pages, which were like a time tablet, have been written on through greater younger infantrymen and preserved their reminiscences, emotions, and studies from the trenches.

Trench battle strategies

Trench conflict used numerous techniques to gain a bonus on this grueling form of combat. Here are some of the maximum well-known strategies.

Trench raids

Under the cover of night time, agencies of squad dies can also sneak into enemy trenches to launch marvel assaults. The attacks needed to be finished with stealth, bravery and speed.

Artillery barrages had been a effective pass that sought to weaken the opponent's defenses. Imagine a stack of weapons unleashing devastating rounds of bullets onto enemy positions. These barrages crammed the air with chaos and destruction that can create openings for infantry assaults.

Gas assaults were an unfortunate truth of trench struggle. Deadly gases like chlorine and mustard gasoline rolled across the land choking and blinding soldiers in their pathway. Gas assaults disrupted plans and induced terror inside the trenches.

Infantry expenses

Soldiers should charge in the course of "no man's land" in an act of bravery. On the battlefield, this region served as a bodily barrier among the ones fighting. Mines, bullets and shrapnel whizzed past infantrymen as they driven ahead to overrun enemy trenches. It has become a excessive-stakes method with a excessive capability payoff. But it additionally carried a excessive opportunity of failure.

Tunneling and mining

Soldiers may dig deep underneath enemy strains to plant explosives under the enemy. But this became a unstable task of cat and mouse. If they were detected then they'll face devastating outcomes.

Innovations in trench war

There were severa dispositions made inside the trenches. Some of the maximum essential ones are summarized under. A more one in every of a type list can be located at the stop of this e-book.

When fuel struggle have become a chief part of the battle, gasoline mask have been invented to shield and shield soldiers from the deadly assaults. First they advanced from simple fabric masks to greater brand new designs to provide life saving protection.

Periscopes allowed squad dies to look the enemy from the safety in their very own trenches. This furnished valuable fact without exposing the squad dies to bullets.

Flamethrowers have been like legendary dragons launching fireside throughout the battlefields. In a blast they may easy enemy troops with terrifying performance. However, protecting one took braveness because of the truth the operator could often be a goal for enemy snipers.

Tanks can also need to steamroll at a few levels inside the battlefield navigating difficult terrain and presenting firepower. Enemy traces were effects beaten beneath them. The appearance of tanks marked a brilliant shift in battlefield dynamics.

Barb twine changed into used as a defense throughout the trenches to hold away enemies. Those unlucky enough to be wrapped up within the jagged edges might be caught inside the sights of enemy fireside.

In this economic break you located approximately the grim realities of trench war. Remember the courage and bravery of the soldiers who fought for their international locations in remote places muddy and threatening lands. In the subsequent bankruptcy we are capable of take a look at all about the heroes lower returned home who supported them.

## Chapter 4: Home Front Heroes

Welcome again all yet again younger historians! So a long way on our revel in via time, we've were given visited the front lines of World War 1 and studied a few clearly remarkable folks who risked their lives to store others. Now we'll take flight to the residence the front, where unsung heroes, women and kids your age executed a important function inside the struggle try.

Take a second to keep in mind what you do every unmarried day. You possibly awaken, cross to school, have a few lunches, do your homework and then lighten up together together with your friends and circle of relatives. Back inside the days of World War 1 children your age moreover followed a comparable habitual. But while the struggle commenced out the whole thing changed inside the blink of an eye fixed Parents had been referred to as away to fight in remote places lands. Meanwhile back inside the homelands children similar to you stepped up in brilliant techniques to useful useful resource their nations and their America human beings stopping foreign places. On the home the front, they set up themselves as a dependable aid tool for the conflict attempt. As you're approximately to look, moreover they showed exceptional resourcefulness and resolution.

(Troops at the home front)

Young heroes at domestic

During World War 1, there were many younger folks who stood up and helped with the struggle try. Firstly they contributed to the gathering of requirements like apparel, blankets or maybe cleaning soap. Even even though they regarded like small contributions, they made a big difference to supporting the soldiers undergo the difficult situations of the conflict. Conditions for squad dies on the front lines were frequently risky and harsh. The sour wintry weather climate continuously bit at them. But the heroes at the residence fronts labored diligently to create comfortable socks and heat scarves. With willpower and care they knitted those heat devices for the soldiers combating an extended manner away from home. With each sew sewn it end up a picture of help and a reminder that there has been someone lower back domestic deliberating them.

Remember that such easy acts of kindness may want to have a large impact. These younger heroes proved that you do not need to be a superhero or positioned on a cape to make a distinction. Even the smallest movements and teamwork can assist to make top notch adjustments.

Through network, compassion and resolution they helped the squaddies foreign places to live robust. All together their moves irrespective of the truth that they regarded small achieved a sizeable characteristic in assisting their nations and the squad dies on the front traces. Allow their recollections to encourage you to usually see opportunities to lend a supporting hand in hard conditions. Every attempt no matter how small can make contributions to a greater cause and make the arena a higher area.

Young spies

In times of warfare statistics is one of the maximum precious weapons. When your enemies strategies and secrets and techniques and techniques it could help to loosen up the keys to victory Spies can help to build up vital facts that could help win wars. With their clever and foxy skills they can sneak at the back of enemy traces to accumulate intelligence and discover hidden secrets and techniques and techniques. Can you imagine being a spy? It wasn't clean, and it changed into very nerve racking. You constantly needed to be steps in advance of the enemy in a bid to outsmart them.

Did you realize that again in World War 1 some of the maximum ambitious spies had been kids? Indeed many had been now not a whole lot older than you! Of course being younger and harmless made them the first-class undercover dealers because of the truth they had been a lot lots less possibly to elevate suspicion. Now allows check a number of the strategies that they spied on the enemies.

On formidable missions they risked being captured on the equal time as amassing information. At all times they had to be quick thinkers and adapt to many surprising situations. Many instances they needed to use all their resourcefulness to interrupt out the stickiest of situations. Each mission became like a puzzle and fixing them required a pointy mind mixed with courage. They were like characters from a exciting journey novel however this emerge as the actual international. They needed to be masters of cowl, rapid capable of take on various identities of newsboys, messengers or maybe college students

Taking pictures changed into an important way of collecting statistics all through the struggle. Young spies photographed touchy statistics about the enemy. These younger spies could sneak up on enemy troops and locations through posing as newsboys or messengers. Then they will ship decrease once more rather useful seen intelligence captured through their cameras.

Another critical tactic those extra youthful spies had been concerned in changed into breaking codes. Together they joined forces with special code breakers to decipher enemy messages. The capability of younger minds to decipher codes and remedy puzzles has emerged as brilliant. Their international locations had been able to better intercept and decipher enemy communications way to the information they accrued.

Remember which you too have a sharp mind and a brave character. Master your abilities and artwork difficult on becoming the brilliant you may be. When the time comes you too will face traumatic conditions however at the side of your enjoy and facts you will without difficulty overcome them.

Children on the house the front

During World War I, extra younger human beings organised diverse groups to reveal harmony with the army and their groups.These golf equipment and adventures were more than just having fun; they were about developing a high-quality impact on the residence the the front.

Meet Olivia, an eleven year antique lady who based totally children for kindness membership in her college. Her membership emerge as all about that specialize in acts of kindness within the form of writing letters to the squad dies and to assist neighbors in want. Her club became a photo of want and a helping hand inside the network that lifted the people's spirits.

Meet Daniel, a fourteen 12 months vintage boy who organized the bicycle brigade. Kids in his gang rode their bicycles to accumulate donations for the infantrymen preventing distant places. Together they peddled through the streets and the parks spreading the objects of generosity everywhere they went. On their trips they helped to raise spirits and vital budget for the soldiers preventing foreign places.

Youths like Olivia and Daniel proved that with creativity and resolution younger humans in the community can become leaders and make a difference. Keep in thoughts that kids your age may be powerful forces for properly as we hold to have a take a look at the lives of our home front heroes. You can also make a difference within the global with the resource of performing some aspect as clean as solving something, beginning a membership or assisting someone else.

Women within the war

At the start of World War 1 ladies had been concerned inside the traditional roles together with staying at home to attend to children and to carry out ordinary home responsibilities. However due to the fact the warfare became more extreme it have end up very easy that extra assist is probably required. Luckily girls had been there to help!

One of the maximum essential roles ladies carried out at some point of World War 1 emerge as nurses. Bravely those women who have been regularly called "the angels of the battlefield" served on the the front lines. There they tended to wounded soldiers with compassion and care. Tirelessly they worked in the region hospitals and risked their lives to maintain others. With dedication and resilience they bravely faced not possible horrors to complete their obligations. Without them topics could in all likelihood were masses worse and it changed into with gratitude that their efforts had been received.

Whilst a few girls labored as nurses others took on equally vital roles collectively with ambulance drivers and medics. Bravely they faced the risks of the battlefield to deliver decrease once more injured squaddies for medical remedy. Courageously those women navigated thru risky conditions to store lives.

Beyond the medical area women additionally served as spies and code breakers. With their sharp minds they proved to be valuable at collecting crucial information and cracking enemy codes. We will in no way comprehend their names because of the truth they worked in thriller but their impactful efforts made a big distinction.

Not all women served on the the front traces but many extra finished an important feature in the battle. Back on the house the front many women performed critical roles together with taking jobs at factories, offices and farms allowing the men who previously labored there to go off to warfare. The girls who remained home took extremely good care to hold a sturdy home the the front and permit the conflict efforts to hold.

Women in World War 1 have become an essential part of our information. Before then they have been no longer dealt with further. The conflict proved that they too are in reality as capable as men. After the struggle in many countries ladies received the proper to vote and feature end up more active in society and politics. Their memories from World War 1 feature a reminder that power and resilience regardless of gender can form the direction of records. Not handiest did they save lives but additionally they set the degree for a greater identical and inclusive destiny. The legacy of those ladies is a testomony to the energy and resolution of breaking down boundaries. Always deal with every precise with fairness irrespective of their records. Our deserves and efforts are what make us and create opportunities for us.

Now the diploma has been set and the heroes had been met. It's time for us to assignment out into a number of the fundamental battles of World War 1. (Storey & Housego, 2010)

## Chapter 5: Western Front

1914 TO 1916

Welcome to a brand new interesting part of our adventure thru the facts of World War 1. Here we are about to go into the primary battles of the battle. Imagine a huge battlefield that protected maximum of Europe. Here, huge armies have to fight fierce and decisive battles in a bid to win the warfare. In those early battles records have become normal within the fires of conflict.

At the begin of World War 1, subjects have been given quite confusing for the Central Powers. They had a plan. But it did not quite workout session the way they predicted. Germany had promised to help Austria-Hungary attack Serbia. However every element had a one-of-a-type concept of what that help need to appear to be. Before the war, the Central Powers had made some plans on the way to combat, however they didn't pass as anticipated. When the conflict started out out it was like they had been gambling a recreation with out information the policies!

(soldiers at the the front strains)

Austria-Hungary perception that Germany must shield them from Russia within the north. But Germany idea Austria-Hungary might cognizance on fighting Russia even as they took care of France within the west. It grow to be like they have been speaking specific languages! This confusion brought on Austria-Hungary to ship its infantrymen to every the Russian and Serbian sides. Overall this can make subjects even greater puzzling and hard for the Central Powers.

The Serbian Adventure

On August twelfth, a few thing important came about inside the land of Serbia.

Austrian and Serb forces fought battles at a place called Cer and every different one at a place referred to as Kolubara. These battles lasted for approximately  weeks. The Austrians hoped for a quick victory, but it did not workout consultation that way due to the fact the Serbs positioned up the sort of robust resistance. The facts disenchanted the Austrians. The Serbs' functionality to save you the Austrians became a large surprise and one of the first instances the countries at the Allies gained a huge fight inside the battle. Because of this, the Austrians needed to hold many squaddies in Serbia, which made it tough for them to combat closer to Russia. (Lyon, 2015)

Something interesting also happened for the duration of this Serbian journey. In the spring of 1915, they used particular guns to shoot down an Austrian aeroplane. That have become the primary time each person had finished that during a struggle. And later inside the fall of 1915 some aspect else outstanding took place. The Serbian forces made a superhero circulate, in which they helped many injured infantrymen with the resource of saving them from the fighting zones. (Miller et al., 2009)

The Big German march

Back in 1914, the German military had a plan to brief take over Belgium and France. With a variety of their squaddies covered up and organized at the Western Front, they hatched a totally precise plan called the Schlieffen Plan. Their leader, Alfred von Schlieffen, concept that they might wonder the alternative component with the resource of going via the Netherlands and Belgium. His plan become to then sweep down and lure the French military close to Switzerland. Ideally, this may take no more than six weeks. From then they may head east to combat Russia.

But, there has been a hassle. After Schlieffen, every other leader named Helmuth von Moltke made a few changes to the plan. He became worried that the French is probably too robust on the left thing. Thus he moved a few soldiers there. Also, he determined no longer to go through the Netherlands because of the truth he desired to maintain them satisfactory for change. (Foley, 2012)

The Germans started out their march and did actually properly on the begin. They even made a number of the Allied forces, which encompass the British retreat. But, then the French released a counter assault in an area referred to as Alsace-Lorraine. It did now not bypass properly for them and they lost many infantrymen which became the tides. As the Germans were given in the direction of Paris they made a mistake.

One in their commanders, von Kluck, failed to follow orders which created a gap among their armies. The French and the British noticed this hollow and stopped the German enhance at a place called the First Battle of the Marne. (Herwig, 2009)

By the give up of 1914, the German squaddies have been deep internal France. They were doing adequate and had taken manipulate of some essential places. However that they had problems with talking to each exquisite and some leaders made some awful choices. They have been moreover being challenged to fight the Russians within the east. This intended they needed to ship critical squaddies far from France to cope with the Russians. Some humans in Germany already knew they had been in trouble and idea they will lose the battle, even though it modified into just beginning.

Tough instances on the the the front lines

When World War 1 started out, the manner armies fought had to alternate. Before then soldiers used to combat in open fields with their rifles. But in 1914, subjects were converting because new generation made it virtually tough to do this. The creation of barbed cord, tool weapons and powerful artillery made it greater tough for soldiers to fight in open fields. Battlefields had grow to be like massive impediment guides. For a while, neither side knew how to break via the ones defences without dropping many squaddies of their efforts. But as time went on new weapons like gas and tanks started out to change the game.

After the First Battle of the Marne, the Allies and the Germans attempted to outflank every first-rate, which intended going across the elements to wonder the enemy. They called this the "Race to the Sea." But by the use of the give up of

1914, they could not skip any similarly and they had to forestall. They stood going through every different with trenches and barbed wire all of the way from the sea to the Swiss border.

The Germans normally held the better ground and had stronger trenches due to the fact they had been given to choose in which they stood. The French and English trenches have been now not as appropriate before the whole lot because of the truth they constructed them thinking they might superb be brief. Their plan had constantly been to interrupt thru the German defences as speedy as feasible.

In 1915, at some point of the Second Battle of Ypres, the Germans did a few trouble virtually scary. They used a toxic fuel called chlorine for the first time in a struggle. From then onwards each factors began out the usage of one in every of a kind gases. This have become a frightening new detail of war that had dire consequences. Along with tanks and innovation the game of battle commenced out to exchange. (Leach, 2016)

For the subsequent  years, neither aspect might also want to win the battle. The British and French out of place greater squaddies than the Germans because of the techniques they attempted to assault. The Germans best launched one big attack, but the Allies made many tries to break thru the German traces.

In 1916, there was a well-known warfare called the Battle of Verdun in which the Germans attempted to seize land, however the French fought decrease again with entire effort. Many soldiers from every sides had been given harm and it in the long run have turn out to be a image of how determined the French have been. (Jankowski, 2014)

Later that twelve months, there has been each different large war known as the Battle of the Somme. The first day of this warfare have end up the deadliest day in British Army records. Many infantrymen were both harm or killed. Overall the conflict delivered about many casualties on all components. Not exceptional did gunshots damage, however life inside the trenches modified into genuinely terrible. Diseases like trench foot, shell surprise, and the 'Spanish flu' made many infantrymen sick. It was a hard time for all and sundry on the the the front strains. (Prior & Wilson, 2016)

As we close to the pages of Chapter 5, we've were given ventured deep into the trenches of World War 1, wherein we have witnessed the relentless struggles, battles and suffering continued via the courageous soldiers. However our exploration of this 2nd in time remains a ways from complete.

For now we are able to bid farewell to the muddy trenches. Next we're approximately to set sail into uncharted waters. Our subsequent voyage will navigate the seas of naval warfare, where powerful warships, sneaky submarines and strategic manoeuvres may come to outline the direction of World War 1.

## Chapter 6: Fighting For Control Of The Seas

We've already located out a exquisite deal about the trenches of World War 1. However our adventure via time is still early on! In this next financial ruin, we can board onto ships, head out to sea and discover a modern day the front inside the naval warfare. In this bankruptcy, we will set sail for a test of the notable naval battles, vessels and legacies of World War 1. Prepare your self to navigate the harmful waters of this historic length wherein ships, submarines and strategic movements fashioned the path of the conflict.

Imagine a large opposition on the excessive seas. But this wasn't about sports or games. No this changed into about a few difficulty a good buy more important! It have end up a race among international locations to gather the most effective fleet of warships. The essential contenders had been the Royal Navy of the United Kingdom and the Imperial Navy of Germany. Huge battles amongst those sea monsters took place on the uneven seas. In the ones battles, warships at the water had been crucial while submarines had been used for thriller surveillance and stealthy attacks.

(U-14 Austro-Hungarian submarine)

A quick Naval facts records

A long time in the past, a leader named Wilhelm preferred his u . S ., Germany, to have a effective navy just like the only in Britain. He surely regarded as much as the British army and desired to be even more potent than them. He perception that if Germany had a sturdy military, the British may not problem Germany in Europe. In the period in-between, Britain finished introduction of the notable-superior deliver HMS Dreadnought. Germany made a first-rate try to capture up however it was tough. This grow to be the overall mood once more while countries were competing to build the most powerful navies. (Hamilton, 2004)

The Battle of Jutland

When World War 1 started at sea, the Battle of Jutland became one of the first and most well-known battles. Everything went down inside the North Sea, no longer far from the coasts of Denmark and Northwest Germany. Several international locations, together with the UK to the west and Denmark, Norway, Sweden, and Germany to the east, surrounded the North Sea. Imagine a massive, bloodless and deep sea that stretches as a long way as your eyes can see. The scene turned into set for a naval conflict of legendary length.

The British Grand Fleet, commanded thru Admiral Sir John Jellico, made up one aspect. The ships beneath his command had been like floating fortresses, armed to the tooth with massive cannons. Facing them on the opposite element have end up the Imperial German High Seas Fleet commanded through Admiral Reinhard Scheer. Under his command emerge as a fleet of German warships that had been further stunning with their very personal effective guns. As these robust navies faced every other, the North Sea have turn out to be about to witness a dramatic conflict.

Now consider the North Sea as a large chessboard. Each warship represented a powerful chess piece. The German and British Admirals were like grand chess masters planning their moves in opposition to every different with precision. On the afternoon of May 31,

1916, combat started out. Each issue changed into making strategic moves in the commencing levels, similar to a chess recreation. The British approach come to be to line up their ships to "circulate the T", a go together with the go with the flow that would direct their cannons on the enemy.

Darkness fell over the ocean because of the reality the solar set. Suddenly, the sky changed into lit up with the aid of the war. Sounds of gunfire echoed thru the night time time time. The sky lit up with cannon fireside like a fireworks display. Scenes of chaos and destruction have been created as shells screamed via the air and crashed into the ships as the sea caught fireside.

Midnight approached and the battle reached a climatic moment. The British Grand Fleet completed an impressive manoeuvre to "move the T" of the German Seas fleet. Executed like a high-quality chess circulate, it placed the British in a dominant position. Suddenly the Germans realised that they had been in intense chance and in order that they skillfully retreated into the cover of darkness. The British Grand Fleet held the benefit however the Germans had managed to get away without suffering a devastating defeat.

The Battle of Jutland have become a brutal, excessive warfare that lasted for hours. When the smoke in the end cleared and dawn broke each factors claimed their very personal victories. Whilst the British had induced greater damage to the Germans, their high seas fleet had additionally taken a few damage. Ultimately the struggle didn't provide a decisive victory for both factor however it did have profound consequences. The British had proved to be effective at blockading Germany and slowly choking off its crucial factors. Meanwhile the Germans had hooked up resilience. (Brooks, 2016)

The Battle of Jutland changed the path of World War 1 in masses of techniques. It brought at the German excessive seas fleet to rethink assignment open warfare and as an alternative recognition on submarine battle. Inevitably, this will motive sports like the sinking of the British steamship Lusitania thru a German U-boat. This claimed the lives of every British and American citizens. These U-boats had attempted to prevent ships from bringing additives to Britain from North America. Sneakily they may attack ships without any warning. This end up really frightening for the human beings on the ones ships due to the fact they did not have lots time to break out. The United States got upset about this and told Germany it wasn't honest. So, Germany modified its recommendations and promised not to assault passenger ships. But Britain did some element awesome. They put guns on their service provider ships and did no longer deliver a caution earlier than firing.

Things commenced out out getting better for the ships in 1917 once they began out touring collectively in agencies known as convoys with destroyers to guard them. This made it difficult for the U-boats to find and attack the ships and it helped lessen the amount of ships that have been given sunk. They furthermore came up (The 2nd battleship squadron of the

German army crusing to the North Sea. Ca. 1911-14.) new strategies to discover and combat the U-boats underwater. It have end up like a endeavor of hide and attempting to find, however with submarines and particular guns. During this time, in addition they commenced out the use of aeroplanes on big ships called plane businesses. These aeroplanes helped them attack important places including aircraft hangars. They even used blimps to search for U-boats underwater. (Gray, 1994)

Ultimately it end up a hard time at sea inside the route of World War 1. Many lives had been misplaced and masses of ships have been destroyed. Let us pay appreciate and keep in thoughts the bravery and sacrifice of all involved. Now we are able to project into Chapter 7 in which smooth adventures, traumatic situations and shifting alliances count on.

## Chapter 7: Fresh Challenges & Southern

As our adventure continues deeper into the tale of World War 1 we now locate ourselves exploring new battlefields. New threats, opponents, enemies and alliances had been starting to emerge. One such mission modified into beginning in the coronary heart of Europe in which Austria-Hungary confronted a huge task. Back in the ones days Austria-Hungary ruled over a substantial empire that included many first-rate international locations. However they had been at the verge of crumble from the load in their many commitments and confined belongings.

After the assassination of Archduke Franz Ferdinand on the hands of a terrorist supported by way of Serbia, Austria-Hungary changed into driven to say its superiority. In an try to weigh down Serbian nationalism, Austria-Hungary determined to punish the united states.

Germany and Austria-Hungary fashioned a powerful enterprise in this conflict. Together they satisfied every different america Bulgaria to sign up for them in struggle in opposition to Serbia. Bulgaria when they were asked to join in did not hesitate, they fast said "do not forget us in".

On October 14th 1915 Bulgaria declared struggle on Serbia. Together they joined forces with the Austrian-Hungarian military which become already in the midst of a big assault concerning over 600 thousand soldiers. Serbia have end up confronted with a difficult venture. Now they needed to combat on factors. The odds have been stacked inside the direction of them and defeat appeared drawing near. With all their might likely they fought toward the large Austria-Hungarian and Bulgarian armies. (Hall, 2014)

The Serbs tried truly tough, but they have been driven all over again within the route of the ocean. In a few different conflict referred to as the Battle of Mojkovac, their buddies from Montenegro helped them. But even that didn't paintings. The Austrians took over Montenegro too. The Serbian squaddies who had been left needed to break out thru sea to Greece or via land into Albania in the south.

Ultimately they were faced with overwhelming forces. Despite their heroic efforts, they virtually couldn't keep at once to their land. The blended electricity of the Bulgarian and Austrian-Hungarian armies modified into sincerely an excessive amount of. After falling, Serbia have come to be then occupied and divided many of the Austro-Hungarian Empire and Bulgaria. However we are capable of revisit them later to see how they got here again from the useless.

## Troubles in Greece

Now permit's leap over to Greece which changed proper right into a neighbouring usa with its non-public percent of troubles sooner or later of this chaotic time. Remember the Allies? Well this remarkable group of nations on the aspect of France and the UK favored to help Greece in the conflict because they believed it'd make a massive distinction. However there was a hitch in the plan.

(ww1 lion memorial in Greece)

King Constantine 1 of Greece became proper friends with Germany of The Central Powers. When the Allies asked for Greece's aid the king wasn't so eager on the concept. So as opposed to teaming up with the Allies he determined to conform with his personal route which did no longer contain turning into a member of them. Like a hurricane on the horizon, an explosive argument erupted over it. As tensions rose, the people of Greece had been now cut up into  camps. One who supported the king, on the equal time as the alternative who sided with the Allies.

The warfare the numerous Allies and the king's forces escalated and it in the end prompted an armed confrontation inside the coronary coronary heart of the Greek capital, Athens. This dramatic event is now remembered as Noemvriana. The king, feeling the warm temperature, determined to step down from his throne and changed into succeeded via his son Alexander in June 1917. Greece now formally joined with the Allies.

With Greece now siding with the Allies the steadiness end up transferring. It changed into a enormous second inside the data of World War 1 which might have a ways attaining outcomes. So steeply-priced readers maintain on for your hats as we input in addition into the epic tale of this global warfare. There's plenty extra research and as you'll fast find out the battle modified into spreading far and big. (Abbott, 2022)

## Macedonia

Now, allow's tour to an area called Macedonia. In the start of World War 1, the combat in Macedonia didn't bypass a awesome deal. But then, some thing critical occurred. A agency of courageous French and Serbian squaddies determined to take over a city known as Bitola in November 1916. It changed right into a honestly hard battle and it value them lots. But they did not surrender and they controlled to seize Bitola. This made matters a hint calmer for some time and it changed into like a small victory inside the center of a large war.

The maximum interesting aspect got here in September 1918. By this time, most of the awful guys from Germany and Austria had left the fight. The Bulgarians, who have been on the lousy element, have been given defeated in a large struggle referred to as Dobro Pole. And through September 25, British and French soldiers had even long long past into Bulgaria itself because the Bulgarian navy become falling aside. Just 4 days later, on September 29, Bulgaria stated they could not combat anymore. (Hall, 2010)

The Germans tried to deliver extra soldiers to forestall them, however they have been too vulnerable to fight lower back. With the fight in Macedonia settled, the way to two massive towns, Budapest and Vienna, became now open for the Allies. The Central Powers knew they could not win anymore, so they determined to make peace. More on that later but for now allow's meet some different big participant within the war.

Italy joins the show

Italy faced a difficult desire to make in the early days of World War 1. Like a referee on the sidelines of a football pastime, they first had no motivation to get worried. The Italian government declared neutrality at the outbreak of conflict, but public opinion modified into divided on the time. The battle went on for masses longer and grew an lousy lot large than genuinely all people had predicted. As the warfare stepped forward it come to be unexpectedly drawing close to its borders and Italy changed into starting to enjoy annoying.

In the early years, Italy had signed a thriller cope with Germany and Austria-Hungary previous to World War 1. However, even as matters escalated, they determined they'll now not persist with this deal. They decided that Austria-Hungary changed into being overly competitive. Disputes over Austro-Hungarian territory wherein Italian have come to be spoken additionally carried out a function. Italy had commonly asserted its right to rule over the ones territories and the Allies had promised Italy those territories in exchange for their help. Public opinion started out to show in favour of the Allies. Furthermore the dangers of doing no longer some thing have become clearer to Italy, so the u . S . Organized for warfare.

When World War 1 began, the Italians concept it became a super risk to make their united states of america more potent. They joined the Allies, because they believed it'd assist them accumulate their dream of a united and stronger Italy. Italy's economic device changed into furthermore suffering at the time. They was hoping to boom their wealth thru international exchange. Italy's get right of entry to into the conflict allowed america to shape alliances with awesome worldwide locations, which could improve monetary increase after the warfare ended. As a give up end result, many Italians observed turning into a member of the battle as a part of a grand approach to increase and decorate their united states of america. They hoped it'd beautify their negotiating role with overseas international locations and motive them to even greater first-rate.

(soldiers in Europe)

Italy had a well-developed military by the time it entered the war in 1915. After careful hobby, Italy decided on to sign up for the battle on the facet that had the splendid chance of triumphing. It have come to be clean that the Allies have been gaining floor and Italy seized the opportunity to sign up for the superb coalition as the conflict dragged on. Their involvement changed the character of the warfare and had far-accomplishing results on every their very personal records and the very last very last results of World War 1.

Battles on the Italian Front

Now it's time for us to enter into the cute landscapes of the Italian the front. This the the front ran thru the lovely Italian Alps, a location with a protracted and storied army facts. Close your eyes and recollect this location complete of rugged mountain peaks and deep valleys in which squaddies travelled thru the treacherous trains. The Italian the the the front rapid superior into a hectic battleground wherein each facets fought for electricity. Time travelers, allow's start our journey to the Italian the the front of World War 1.

The Italian Front turn out to be a brand new the the the front that standard in the Alpine region after Italy joined the Allies in May 1915. Picture a fierce warfare taking region a number of the jagged peaks of the Alps, with Italian soldiers of their olive green uniforms. The battles on this the the front worried excessive stakes video video games of outwitting and outmanoeuvring the enemy. The lovely but unforgiving landscapes served due to the reality the backdrop for the stories of bravery and sacrifice, from the bloody Battle of Caporetto to the heroic defence at the Battle of Monte Grappa. (Marcuzzi, 2020)

The battles on the Italian the the front have been extended and brutal. Many ended in extended stalemates that in the end contributed to sporting down the Central Powers. In addition it took a massive financial stress on all forces involved. The rate of constructing armies and bases in tough terrains tired sources that might have been used for different purposes. The Italian the front became a very unique second in World War 1 wherein the soldiers weren't simply stopping the enemy however they were struggling with the factors as properly. They have been faced with snow protected peaks, icy winds, avalanches and perilous enemies. In mountain battle frostbite and altitude contamination had been truely as lethal because of the reality the enemy's bullets. Not handiest did they face unstable enemies but they also faced survival in a number of the area's most hard situations. The mountainous terrain of the Italian Front turn out to be a completely unique undertaking for each elements. It required incredible resources for constructing bases, supply traces and sending troops to the mountains wherein that needed to acclimatise. This drain on assets become a problem for every Italy and Austria-Hungary and it had extra consequences inside the stability of energy of the conflict.

As a result of Italy's get admission to into the battle, the Central Powers, led via Austria-Hungary, were pressured to redirect an huge quantity of their army and property inside the course of securing their southern borders. However, the military forces of these international locations had been already being placed to heavy use at the Eastern and Western Fronts. Now they needed to cut up those forces to stand the Italians. Because of this, Austria-Hungary become put beneath first rate strain because it had to shield a tough terrain from Italian attacks. The Central Powers should have used those sources some area else, however strengthening the Italian Front become a need to. As a cease result, the Central Powers' method became weakened and

Austria-Hungary grow to be now not able to release large assaults some other place. Ultimately, it swung the chances in favour of the Allies and tipped the stableness of energy to them. The Central Powers' isolation have become deepened as a latest powerful high-quality friend in Italy joined closer to their coalition.

## Chapter 8: The Ottoman Empire

As the struggle advanced, it blanketed new territories and drew in additional international places. With World War 1 as a backdrop, this chapter will now take us into the charming global of the Ottoman Empire, where alliances shifted and battles for manage spread out. For more than six centuries, the Ottoman Empire had ruled over a big territory. Located on the crossroads of Europe, Asia and Africa it has become a enormous participant in the information of the world. It changed into virtually, genuinely massive and blanketed

3 continents! In Europe it covered southeastern Europe with territories within the Balkans and Greece. In Asia maximum of the empire grow to be placed in modern day Turkey, areas of the Middle East and elements of western Asia. Even in Africa elements of the empire have been placed in Libya, Egypt and Sudan.

(Whirling Dervishes in Istanbul, Turkey - Ottoman Empire)

Historical Background

The Ottoman Empire originated inside the early 14th century while it become based through the use of Osman 1 from whom the Empire took its name. Originally it emerged from the Byzantine Empire and over time extended thru navy conquests, global relations and strategic alliances. As the centuries surpassed it have emerge as one of the most effective and mythical empires in history. (Editors, 2019)

In the early years of World War 1 the Ottoman Empire turns out to be led via the bold management of the Young Turks. The Young Turks preferred to replace the Ottoman Empire's absolute monarchy with a ultra-modern constitutional authorities. A turning component in its facts happened at some stage in World War 1. Initially taking a unbiased stance, the Ottoman Empire in the end joined forces with Germany and Austria-Hungary to shape The Central Powers. But it'd grow to be being a bad preference with some distance-attaining results. (Turfan, 2000)

Gallipoli Campaign

Now let's get on a deliver and head to the lovely Ottoman Peninsula of Gallipoli. The sea and the past meet at this point in time. The Allies, which blanketed forces from Australia and New Zealand, were plotting an attack in opposition to The Central Powers inside the Ottoman Empire.

Soldiers in this advertising advertising marketing campaign might adopt a formidable assignment, storming seashores and crossing perilous cliffs and trenches.

Brave soldiers from Australia and New Zealand embarked on a ambitious journey to break the stalemate that had gripped the Western Front for goodbye. Like knights in shining armour they stepped into the unknown with the preference of turning the tides of struggle of their favour. But it would come at a super rate. The Gallipoli Peninsula modified into a risky and rocky terrain protected with the useful resource of fierce and decided Ottoman defenders.

In April 1915 the bold and audacious plan commenced out out to unfold. Allied forces together with the Australian and New Zealand corps (ANZAC) released into an bold, amphibious assault on The

Gallipoli Peninsula. Their undertaking changed into to everyday the beaches and set up a foothold in an area that become complete of uncertainty and demanding conditions. This provided massive stressful conditions from the begin. (McLean, 2009)

The Gallipoli Peninsula end up a rugged and rocky landscape that made it as an opportunity difficult for troops to move through. Rocky beaches and steep cliffs added to the complexity in their assault. Furthermore, the Ottomans had located up a fierce defence beneath the control of Mustafa Kemal Atatürk, later the founding father of current Turkey. His forces have been despatched to the Peninsula with strength of will to shield their region of starting. Against them The Allies additionally needed to cope with harsh climate situations beginning from scorching heat inside the summer time to the bitter cold of the winter. Combined with constrained property and components it proved to be a totally difficult assignment.

Despite preliminary successes the campaign soon have come to be an extended drawn out challenge resulting in a stalemate. Both facets determined themselves in a situation that become turning into worse with the aid of the day. The ANZAC troops along the British and the French continued unbelievable conditions and suffered heavy casualties. In a few situations they had been even concerned in brutal hand-to-hand fight. The Gallipoli advertising advertising and marketing campaign have emerge as a image of courage and resolution. Both factors confirmed remarkable bravery inside the face of adversity incomes the honour and admiration of their comrades.

The marketing marketing campaign dragged on for eight extended months and neither thing became able to stable a victory. By December 1915 the Allied forces noticed the futility of the situation and decided to evacuate from The Gallipoli. For the Ottoman Empire the a hit defence of their terrain closer to distant places invasion contributed to the eventual basis of present day-day Turkey. Mustafa Kemal Atatürk's management need to emerge as a defining economic disaster in that information. The Gallipoli advertising campaign in the long run stays a powerful financial spoil inside the records of World War 1 marked with the aid of the use of valour, sacrifice and the memories of individuals who fell on its rocky seashores.

The Armenian Genocide

As we maintain our journey thru time, we are capable to investigate more approximately the Ottoman Empire's involvement in World War 1. The

Armenian Genocide is a tragic financial disaster in the data of human suffering that we should now confront.

Armenia have become a land of wealthy subculture and history. Located inside the South Caucasus vicinity of Western Asia deep inside the Ottoman Empire. In current-day day terms it changed into nestled amongst Turkey to the west, Georgia to the north, Azerbaijan to the east and Iran to the South. Armenia has a protracted data that stretches decrease lower back hundreds of years with exceptional contributions to artwork, literature and religion.

Now let us flip our attention to this deeply sombre financial catastrophe in the history of the Armenian humans. This financial ruin spread out within the borders of the Ottoman Empire in which a shadow descended upon the Armenian population. It changed right right into a shadow of cruelty and struggling which have emerge as a stark assessment to the colourful way of lifestyles those human beings had celebrated for generations.

The Armenian Genocide end up a coronary heart-wrenching tail of tragedy wherein mass deportations, violence and struggling befell. It have become as although a hurricane had swept thru the ones peoples lives pushing out families from their homes, tearing aside companies and subjecting harmless people to not possible hardships.

(Armenian Genocide. Tsitsernakaberd Memorial Complex)

Families were forcibly separated, their houses were taken over and their lives had been forever changed. Armenians who had lengthy been a treasured part of the Ottoman Empire's numerous subculture had been treated as outcasts and had been each thrown out or killed. But why?

Several factors contributed to the Armenian Genocide. The Armenians had been a super Christian minority in a predominantly Muslim Ottoman Empire. This created a religious divide that had lengthy and complex historic roots. As the Ottoman Empire struggled with internal strife and territorial losses a experience of nationalism grew among ethnic companies.

The Armenian population changed into seen as a capability chance because of their ethnic identity and aspirations for autonomy. Furthermore the Ottoman Empire at some stage in World War 1 preferred to secure its eastern borderlands and prevent functionality collaborations a number of the Armenians and the Ottoman Empire's enemies including Russia. Ultimately World War 1 ignited the tensions even extra and because the battle waged on, the Ottoman Empire engaged in mass deportations, violence and atrocities toward the Armenian population. The enduring instructions from this financial disaster feature a harsh reminder to the horrors that may unfold even as hatred and intolerance are allowed to flourish unchecked. As seekers of knowledge and historians we must research from it and paintings in the direction of a better future. (Kévorkian, 2011)

As the struggle dragged on the Ottoman Empire persevered to face inner strife in addition to outside threats. Forevermore its roots were weakened by manner of World War 1. Ultimately this had set in movement its eventual crumble and the beginning of new worldwide places in its wake.

## Chapter 9: Adventures In The East
## Heroes, Changes, And Big Battles

The next prevent on our excursion throughout the battlefields of World War 1 lands us in Eastern Europe. More game enthusiasts had been about to go into into the motion. In this bankruptcy, we are able to find out approximately Romania's role in World War 1, the consequences and one of a kind critical moments at the Eastern Front. Moreover, we are able to go through witness to the emergence of the large Russian huge, whose get entry to into the conflict ought to for all time alter the path of records.

Picture the huge area of Eastern Europe due to the fact the backdrop, wherein the Carpathian Mountains stand tall like giants and the Danube River flows speedy and furiously. It's proper here that we will find the top notch tale of Romania's courageous infantrymen, who stepped onto the area degree with hopes of making their mark. We'll observe their battles and the effect that that that they had on a complex community of alliances and rivalries.

The Eastern the the front of World War 1 extended a ways all through Eastern Europe. Picture a map of Europe and visualise a line that stretches from the Baltic Sea in the north to the Black Sea in the south. This line represented the the front line of the Eastern Front and it's far an area that blanketed current-day Poland, Ukraine, Belarus, the Baltic states, Russia and Romania. Military operations in the area were complex via the huge fashion of languages and cultures there.

Close your eyes and consider this panorama that tiers from the sweeping planes of Russia to the rugged Carpathian mountains of the Czech Republic to Romania. Armies were tasked with manoeuvring through thick forests, crossing powerful rivers and enduring harsh winters. Nations sought to protect their pursuits, assert their dominance and emerge powerful in the transferring alliances of World War 1.

Romania

Romania, a rustic in Eastern Europe, confronted a crucial choice in 1916, throughout World War 1. Two choices lay earlier than them. Option one became to organization up with the Allies, a hard and fast of first-class worldwide places just like the United Kingdom, France and Russia. These buddies promised Romania land and assist. Option became to enroll within the Central Powers, led thru manner of Germany and Austria-Hungary, who they had been once remarkable with. Romania's leaders notion in truth difficult and decided to go together with the Allies. This have become unusual as it meant they've come to be pals with the nations they was closer to. Such a choice changed into a large deal and it'd trade matters for Romania in lots of strategies.

Romania's borders have grow to be a big battlefield in the sport of conflict. Romanian infantrymen went on particular missions for the duration of the huge battles. One assignment worried saving a place called Transylvania, wherein many Romanians lived. But bet what? Hungary, part of a place known as the Austro-Hungarian empire, managed it. Romanian infantrymen had been first-rate brave. They climbed mountains and fought actually tough to assist their human beings in Transylvania. It became hard, but they did not surrender. Their courage confirmed how strong they have been and it made a massive difference.

Another frontline opened in Moldova wherein Romanian forces faced huge armies from the Central Powers. On the banks of the Siret and Prut rivers fierce battles have been fought as Romania defended its territory and glued by using manner of their dedication to the Allied cause. The Siret and Prut rivers served as countrywide barriers and protecting positions for Romanian forces. Along the ones waterways Romanian squaddies displayed a courageous willpower to protect their homelands.

The Central Powers, in the interim, have been making moves to boost their manipulate over essential territory and property in the vicinity. The preventing alongside this the the the front line have end up especially fierce and hard. Extreme climate, a loss of substances, and the regular worry of enemy attacks were surely a number of the many challenges faced with the useful resource of way of squaddies on every elements. The bravery and perseverance of folks that fought in this front, in addition to the suffering of those who lived nearby have become legendary.

Eastern Europe have come to be a complicated chessboard of shifting alliances and goals after Romania's whole get entry to into the struggle. The already demanding historical scenario inside the area changed into further complicated through becoming a member of the Allies. Ultimately their involvement within the conflict had a top notch effect on the Eastern Front. As a cease give up end result of sturdy competitors led through Russia at the Eastern Front, the Central Powers were weakened as they were pressured to shift greater property from the Western Front. Forced to commit troops and assets, the Central Powers' Romanian advertising marketing campaign altered the close by balance of energy in Eastern Europe.

As we pass ahead in our exploration of World War 1, it's miles important that we never forget about the contributions of nations like Romania. Those who fought on the front lines and helped at domestic had been critical in turning the tide of the warfare. (Torrey, 1998)

Russia

One of the defining abilties of the Eastern Front modified into the huge mobilisation of the Russian Empire. Imagine a big go through developing from an prolonged sleep. This end up form of the manner it felt at the same time as lots of Russian infantrymen had been awakened from their sleep. During the height of the Russian Empire's recruitment pressure and because of its huge populace, Russia modified into capable of construct big armies. Ultimately this will be a workout changer.

(German military advancing on Russia)

But why did Russia select out to enroll in the Allies? Well Russia had a few buddies inside the Allies' organization, like France and Britain. These buddies talked to Russia and requested for assist in the conflict. Just like when your buddies ask you to play together, Russia decided directly to beneficial aid its friends.

Furthermore, Germany in the different group, the Central Powers, have end up not so exceptional with Russia. They had already had many disagreements and strength struggles. Russia additionally desired to help its pal Serbia, which have become being bullied by means of way of the use of any other usa known as Austria-Hungary. They too had been part of the Central Powers walking with Germany. In addition Russia favored to advantage extra land. They concept being within the struggle at the Allies factor ought to help them gain extra land.

Russia's get right of access to into the battle had a massive effect at the dynamics of the Eastern the the the front. They have been able to release massive offensives on multiple fronts, pressuring the Central Powers which embody Germany, Austria-Hungary and the Ottoman Empire. The sheer scale of the Eastern Front made it hard for the Central Powers to mount a a hit defence. Their battles alongside the Eastern Front blanketed many crucial ones that original its course in records. Here are a number of the most famous ones.

Battle of Tannenberg

In the early days of World War I the Battle of Tannenberg turned into a vital second on the Eastern the the front. The German navy beneath the incredible control of General Paul Von Hindenburg and his leader personnel, General Erich Ludendorff made strategic moves that could echo at some point of records.

In the early tiers of the battle the Russian Empire released an offensive into East Prussia, a area that become then part of Germany. The Russians consider to brief become German territory, however General Hindenburg on the side of Ludendorff completed a masterful approach. Imagine them orchestrating the defence like expert conductors crucial an orchestra.

The German forces lured the Russians proper right into a lure close to Tannenberg this is contemporary-day Poland. It turn out to be shape of like putting a snare for a massive go through to stroll into. Here the German navy surrounded the Russian forces putting aside them from reinforcements and deliver lines. Thousands of Russian squaddies were taken prisoner and their boom into East Prussia changed into halted which led to a decisive victory for the Germans. (Jordan & Neiberg, 2014)

Gorlice-Tarnów Offensive

In 1915, German and Austro-Hungarian forces released a massive attack on the Eastern Front, focusing their efforts at the Gorlice-Tarnów area in present-day Poland. This turn out to be an brilliant comeback in a traumatic scenario. After a period of quiet, it suddenly have grow to be as severe as a thunderstorm. Gas struggle modified into one of the Central Powers' horrible new techniques that helped them breach the Russian lines. The Russians were compelled to withdraw because of this offensive, which marked a decisive shift in the stability of strength on the Eastern Front. Overall, this offensive had a extraordinary effect, moving the stability of energy and increasing the depth of the warfare on the Eastern Front. (DiNardo, 2010)

The Brusilov Offensive

Now speedy ahead to 1916 and bear in mind a massive hurricane that become accumulating on the Eastern Front. Russia beneath the command of General Alexei Brusilov launched a huge and nicely-planned attack in opposition to the Central Powers. This become like a thunderous roar that shook the recommendations of the Austria-Hungarian empire.

Brusilov's undertaking changed into speculated to be a distraction, but it fee the Russian army dearly. In order to break through the enemy traces, Brusilov had smaller corporations of Russian soldiers assault the enemy's weaknesses. This turned into in assessment to the ordinary army tactic of the time, which involved sending big numbers of troops in a single pass. On the Western Front, generals from France, Germany, and Britain all used similar techniques. They hired those techniques at a conflict called Verdun. In subsequent instances, the Germans made giant use of them, with top notch results.

Ultimately the Brusilov Offensive is remembered as one of the deadliest battles in history. Sadly, many humans were given harm on this project. Russia suffered nearly one million casualties. Austria-Hungary and Germany additionally had many casualties, once more almost one million. Looking returned, it is clean that Russia did properly on this challenge but ultimately did now not preserve up its momentum. The Russian humans have been given discouraged and stopped believing their leaders can also want to win the war. Hard instances had begun for the Russian Empire. The populace become ill of the warfare and their leaders and demanded a alternate in government. The avenue now brought approximately the tail surrender of World War 1 and the turbulence of the Russian Revolution. (Dowling, 2008)

The Russian Revolution

In 1917 Russia changed into beginning to go through fundamental modifications. It felt like pieces of a big puzzle had been being taken apart and located lower again collectively in absolutely new preparations. The Russian Revolution became a huge event that modified into approximately to have outcomes in the path of the significant charges of the Russian Empire. In truth it would be felt all of the manner throughout the landscape of World War 1.

Whilst World War 1 changed into nonetheless taking place, some thing very important befell in Russia. In February 1917, there was a revolution in Russia referred to as the "February Revolution." People have been so bored to death with the manner their usa have become being run that they decided they not preferred a monarchy. Just like in a fairy tale at the same time as an evil king or queen is deposed, they ordered the royal couple to go away america of a.

In October 1917 a few different interesting issue occurred, known as the "October Revolution." The authorities grow to be overthrown presently with the beneficial aid of a collection headed by using manner of using Vladimir Lenin. Bolsheviks turn out to be the decision given to them. To all appearances, that they had a cutting-edge technique for leading the kingdom. Meanwhile with the rest of the arena caught up in World War 1, Russia underwent all of those changes. Not simplest changed into there a high battle, however Russia was moreover present technique sizable modifications and adventures of its very very own. You couldn't have picked a more big generation in statistics! (Riasanovsky & Watson, 1991)

Now the modifications have been now not limited to certainly politics. Changes extended deep into society, way of life and even the material of ordinary lifestyles. The vintage strategies of existence and hierarchies had been challenged with a contemporary generation that became dawning. Imagine it like a big wave sweeping out the antique techniques and bringing within the new. This changed into a duration of each satisfaction and uncertainty in which humans have been faced with big adjustments taking place spherical them on a every day foundation. This financial smash of revolution and change in Russia modified into an vital second now not simplest in the u.S.A.'s history but moreover the outcomes of World War 1. A new technology have become unfolding as the world watched with anticipation to see how the ones changes would possibly effect the warfare's very last tiers.

For the infantrymen stopping at the Eastern fronts the modifications had direct results. The Russian navy, which grow to be as soon as a powerful strain, have become now in chaos. Soldiers had been leaving the the the front lines to enroll in the revolutionaries decrease decrease lower back home. Discipline had fallen off as had the capability to mount powerful offensives. The Central Powers appreciably Germany discovered this as an possibility. With Russia ate up thru the revolution, the

Central Powers shifted their forces to the Western Front in a bid for a decisive victory there. On the grand chessboard one facet had all at once withdrawn some of their portions which now created opportunities for his or her opponent at the board. (McMeekin, 2017)

Lenin's Bold Move

Vladimir Lenin and the Bolshevik Party had a modern vision for Russia after seizing electricity within the metropolis of Petrograd. It have become like a magic trick, except in place of generating a rabbit from a hat, their intention become to get Russia out of World War 1.

Lenin and his institution had been nicely aware about the devastating consequences the conflict modified into having on Russia and its human beings. So, they came up with a cutting-edge-day plan. They signed the "Treaty of Brest-

Litovsk" with the Central Powers (Germany and Austria-Hungary) in March of 1918. This became a definitely formidable step! When they signed this treaty, it formally intended that Russia turn out to be now not a part of World War 1. It changed into like pronouncing, "We're performed with this battle." And due to the fact the ink dried on that agreement, some issue super passed off at the map of the conflict. The stopping at the Eastern Front, wherein Russia emerges as, stopped too. (Magnes, 1919)

When Russia left the struggle it created a dominant impact at the Eastern the the front. The Central Powers may additionally need to now shift their forces to the Western Front in which they sought a decisive victory. The withdrawal of Russia moreover created possibilities for emblem spanking new worldwide locations that emerged in its wake alongside Ukraine and the Baltic States to end up greater independent. These adjustments hold to have influences as much as the current.

With the Russian Revolution withdrawal we now circulate into the very last years of World War 1. The struggle became however raging and as we embark at the very last leg of our journey we'll find out how antique it evolved and in the end concluded. So high-priced time web page traffic, fasten your seatbelts as we adventure thru the turbulent very last years of World War 1.

## Chapter 10: The First Battle Of The Marne

Germany, knowing it'd probably face enemies on elements, devised a plan to defeat France speedy so they'll turn their hobby to Russia, which changed into predicted to take longer to mobilize a navy. Because the border among France and Germany end up carefully fortified, on the night time of August third, 1914, German forces (in a approach called the Schrieffer Plan, named for Alfred Graf von Schrieffer, a former German commander) as an possibility marched into Belgium, planning to attack France from the north and subdue the u . S. A. Inside six weeks.

However, independent Belgium had an agreement with Britain, in which Britain have become dedicated to defensive Belgium. British forces entered the conflict and shortly arrived in France. Within days, all European worldwide places are concerned, besides for Italy, which had signed a neutrality settlement with France.

For the primary few weeks, the Germans superior and moved south into France The reason have end up to transport quick through Belgium with a large stress and turn south after which east in a decisive offensive that could curl in the back of the French troops amassed close to the German border, after which preserve southward to subdue Paris. Unfortunately, the modern-day-day commander, Chief of Staff Helmuth von Moltke, had encompass fewer troops than were within the real method, having sent seven divisions closer to Antwerp. This changed into one element said within the failure of the plan, afterward.

The Battle

Northeast of Paris, near the Marne River, the Germans met the French Sixth Army underneath Commander-in-Chief Joseph Joffre and commanded with the resource of the usage of Michel-Joseph Maunoury. On September 6th and seventh, reinforcements arrived—3000 squaddies have been transported to the the the front in 600 taxis from Paris—the first time a big kind of troops had been moved thru motorized cars.

Faced with opposition, the German First Army have grow to be too brief in the route of the east, exposing the proper flank of their forces to defenders—the French Sixth Army—out of doors Paris.

Having also outpaced his deliver line, Van Moltke decided to barren region the

Schlieffen Plan, retreat, and bypass south to strike Verdun. He hoped to save you counterattacks with the resource of French forces, however it changed into too past due. As the German First Army had became to satisfy their attackers to the west, an opening have been opened among the First and Second German armies, and the Allies were capable of take benefit of it. Hearing reviews of troops getting into the distance, the Second German Army end up ordered to retreat, with a fashionable retreat starting the next day.

Six French armies and the British Expeditionary Forces beneath Field Marshal Sir John French pushed the Germans returned, in which they dug themselves in. Thus started 4 years of trench war, and the stop of the German aspirations for a fast victory in France.

The Outcome

This early principal battle of the warfare changed into a highly-priced one that lasted from September sixth to September twelfth, 1914.It marked a turning element in which the German provide a lift to into France come to be ended and the fighters took to the trenches they will inhabit for the subsequent 4 lengthy years, with little gained or misplaced throughout that time. The outcome of this war would probable have political repercussions for many years to return.

Two million guys fought inside the battle of the Marne. Casualties from the struggle are said to be 227,000 on the French facet (31,376 deaths), and 256,000 at the German aspect, with an anticipated sixty seven,000 killed. No other struggle of WWI need to see such quite a few injuries according to day.

At the outbreak of the battle, military leaders expected that new technology have become going to assist them win battles, but in reality, new inclinations like tool weapons had been extra useful in shielding territory than in overtaking it. Even motorized motors like vehicles had been of confined use for offensive maneuvers for the purpose that they required roads and the land changed into often torn other than war. (Tanks might in all likelihood no longer come into use until later.)

Strategically, the warfare have turn out to be a victory for the Triple Entente. Paris had been defended from the Germans, and the German retreat had fee them nearly 12,000 prisoners, a hundred device guns, and 30 place guns. Helmuth von Moltke became brushed off.

## The Battle of the Somme

### No Man's Land

After the first battles of the warfare to give up all wars, the trenches—and the destruction that lay amongst them—have become a everlasting feature of the struggle. Barbed twine, mud, mounded earth, human stays, mines, and abandoned device lay strewn for miles and miles in an unsightly gash within the course of the French nation-state from the English channel all of the way to Switzerland, nonetheless jealously contested in lots of places thru warring armies. All vegetation has ended up prolonged beyond. It grow to be a desolate—and pretty dangerous—region.

The Battle

In January 1916, little improvement had been made in a 12 months, and the opposing forces had been dug into 450 miles of trenches going through each different throughout this muddy hell. The Entente became attempting to find to get the north of France and Belgium back from the Germans, to which stop Sir Douglas Haig and Joseph Joffre planned a summer season offensive. They knew they may want loads of fellows—the trenches continually desired the defenders.

In February, the Germans attacked the fortress at Verdun. All French reserves had been sent there to protect the city, so whilst summer season came, it fell to the British to persuade the warfare at the

Somme, now with the added aim of relieving the strain at the French with the aid of using drawing stopping forces away from Verdun.

British Field Marshal Haig should have preferred to have interaction the Germans farther north, close to Ypres, but the British and French strains came together near the Somme, just so was wherein the battle would probable take location. To prepare, the commanders set approximately stockpiling weapons and ammunition, and troops. They additionally built roads and railways.

Unfortunately, on this vicinity, the Germans had strong defenses with protective traces and a 3rd inside the method of being built in the once more of them. Each line of protection have come to be made from 3 rows of trenches— fireside, assist, and reserve, with communication trenches becoming a member of them. Many system gun positions had been set up, and there had been fortified cities and villages alongside the route, in addition to deep dugouts to shield the troops from artillery hearth. Phone lines furnished rapid communique, and the troops had been nicely-professional.

The British Fourth Army (made from civilian volunteers) is probably led through way of Sir Henry Rawlinson. He and Douglas Haig had decided that the British may release every week-prolonged artillery attack with 1400 weapons to ruin barbed twine, collapse trenches, and kill soldiers. Nineteen mines were dug in strategic positions and filled with explosives.

Finally, within the north, the British Third military may additionally create a diversion at Gomme court, at some stage in which the British and French infantries may additionally go with the flow closer to their dreams.

The week-lengthy assault happened, and earlier than the whole lot, the men were confident. But due to the gunners' loss of experience, now not enough heavy guns, and faulty shells, hundreds of the barbed cord remained in area. The German infantry of their trenches become regularly unhurt, and due to the reality they'd taken captives and had get proper of get right of entry to to to un-coded mobile smartphone communications, the Germans knew exactly what the British were as a whole lot as.

On the morning of July 1st, the British blew up the German function at Hawthorne Redoubt and the infantry moved to take the location, searching in advance to that the manner have been cleared. Up and down the line, more positions were attacked with explosives.

The Allied troops moved in the direction of the second one line in the course of no guy's land, trying to get through gaps in the barbed twine. Unfortunately, because of the fact the preliminary assault became no longer as a achievement as that that they had was hoping, the Germans had been in a function to protect the ditch and most of the British and French had been shot, mainly in regions wherein they crowded into openings in the barbed twine.

In some areas inside the north, British troops were capable of take German positions, which consist of the Schwaben and Leipzig Redoubts, in addition to the Lochnagar crater—but without any guide, they have been now not capable of hold the ones earnings.

In the south, the Germans were a whole lot less properly prepared, so a number of the French troops have been able to advantage ground, supported via French heavy weapons, which were more powerful at destroying barbed wire.

By 9:30 am, south of the Somme, the French had executed their targets, but within the north, the British had in massive component failed. The Germans suffered 12,000 casualties, the French, 7,000, and the British had 57,000 casualties—a 3rd of them killed—making nowadays the bloodiest day within the British Army. And it wasn't over.

In August, the British landed in France with 40 nine of their new armored tanks, by no means earlier than visible despite the useful resource of the British troops. Some have become mired within the dust, but a few were given thru and have been able to roll over the barbed wire or even the trenches. The Germans fled in terror. Unfortunately, there weren't enough tanks, and the British were no longer prepared with enough guys to hurry in and take benefit of the surprise.

One of the vital disturbing situations at some stage in WWI come to be getting actual-time information from the battlefront to the commanders. Messengers, flags, and lighting had been used, and on fair days, blimps and airplanes may moreover need to collect very precious records about how topics were playing out.

Since they couldn't rely upon verbal exchange from the the front, the waves of a struggle plan were set to a schedule, with heavy armor firing and help devices advancing at timed periods. It often passed off that the infantry modified into now not able to preserve up with the artillery, and this brought on many techniques to transport awry. Leadership frequently didn't understand for hours— or maybe days—which attacks were a success. Most of the time, devices relied on a way of blasting enemy trenches with artillery to try and weaken their opponent after which sending waves of guys on foot to attempt to seize those trenches.

Consequently, the warfare may additionally maintain for a few special 4 months. The surrender of battle started out on November thirteen, with the Battle of the Ancre, and it end up depressing. Field Marshal Douglas Haig resolved to take four villages on the excessive ground of Le Transloy Ridge earlier than halting their operations for the wintry climate.

Rain over the last weeks had made the ground a big rest room, and there was a layer of ice on pinnacle. These were terrible conditions for the five divisions of infantry worried; there was sleet and snow that devilled the men and occasional clouds made air reconnaissance now not feasible. It grow to be almost no longer feasible to move the artillery via the mess.

On November 13, Britain's Fifth Army underneath General Sir Hubert Gough have become able to take of the villages. On the 14th, they won the 1/three. They determined they may make one extra push within the path of the final purpose on the 18th, at some point of which they did benefit a touch floor—but it didn't remember plenty. After suffering 20,000 extra casualties, Haig and the British command sooner or later determined that the Somme offensive modified into not going to art work.

The Germans agreed, and inside the spring, they drew all over again to the Hindenburg line to avoid any extra preventing on the Somme.

In all, the British and French may take 10 miles of territory, in the route of which

Germany suffered 450,000 casualties, the French   hundred,000, and the British 430,000.

The Outcome

In Britain, the Battle of the Somme became seen as a needless catastrophe. In truth, in August 1916 whilst the war were taking place for a month, Winston Churchill—head of the War Committee in Britain at that factor—wrote a letter expressing his dismay that the British had made so little improvement regardless of losing extra men than the Germans had. This contemporary sentiment continued in Britain, even after the war.

But in Europe, the Battle of the Somme seemed like a success. The British did assist to defend the French, who have been then able to beat the Germans at Verdun. And they located out masses about a way to fight in the trenches of the western front.

The use of tanks, on the identical time as admittedly being a constrained success, did offer a state-of-the-art way for navy strategists to bear in mind trench battle, which have been a stubborn puzzle till now. After the Battle of the Somme, greater advanced prototypes is probably advanced the use of the training located out here. This may also lead to research and improvement on anti-tank guns. A new generation commenced.

In all, the Battle of the Somme became to be one of the most devastating conflicts of the conflict, with over one million casualties. Many towns and villages in the place were destroyed, as became enterprise infrastructure, not to say the land itself, which although bears the mark one hundred years later.

The loss of life and destruction of this conflict additionally live on in human memory while we think about the terrible situations and lack of life and limb that characterized World War I.

The Battle of Verdun

The longest and one of the deadliest battles of the war fought a number of the French and German armies

In past due 1915, every elements of the struggle were searching to break the stalemate that persevered on the western the front. After a twelve months of trench warfare, numerous big offensives on each components had already failed, and now the French and British have been focused on a developing battlefront along the Somme, farther to the north.

German Chief of Staff Erich von Falkenhayn believed that Russia need to unavoidably fall and Italy stood little risk of getting a extremely good deal effect at the outcome of the war; France come to be the actual impediment. If France can be defeated, the struggle might be acquired. He proposed attacking Verdun, a city in western France. Verdun were a number one French stronghold from the time of the Romans, due to its herbal defenses. By this time, it had a protective ring of fortresses built after the Franco-Prussian warfare, in addition to particular forts and bunkers.

Taking the town may want to offer the Germans a sturdy advantage, but that wasn't Falkenhayn's crucial goal. He knew the French need to need to defend the city at any fee, so his plan turned into to maintain attacking and permit the French use up their troops in a battle of attrition. He preferred to create horror, an assault so immoderate that the French to experience there was no get away. He said, "No line is to live unbombarded, no opportunities of deliver unmolested, nowhere want to the enemy experience himself consistent."

Behind the rugged panorama and the use of planes as a distraction, for weeks the Germans constructed concrete bunkers and railways for the 1300 munitions trains that would supply combatants on the the front with over million shells. Because this vicinity had no longer up to now been a high a part of the fighting, the French had been unaware of what turn out to be taking place.

The assault started out out on February 21st, 1916. Long-distance German weapons began out bombarding the city from out of doors its ring of fortifications, hitting the bishop's palace and unfavorable the cathedral. For 9 hours, the Germans hammered the allies with 1220 guns on 12 ½ miles along the Meuse River.

A million shells were fired, and the conflict can be heard one hundred miles away. The ground emerge as torn apart, and the incessant roar of the guns grow to be maddening.

By eight:00 a.M., all French phone communications had been lessen off, no reinforcements had been coming, and the commanders were at a loss. The Germans even deployed 168 planes—the maximum crucial aerial net to date—to save you French planes from getting a revel in of what became taking vicinity.

At four:00 p.M. The assault ended, and the German infantry marched in competition to the French.

The destruction have become high-quality. One corporal remarked that out of every 5 guys, "two were buried alive beneath their shelter,  are wounded, and the fifth is prepared."

On day , the Germans superior  miles with the assist of 96 flamethrowers. They took 3000 French prisoners. In the chaos, they superior, but the French did no longer retreat.

On February 24th, the Germans broke via the French strains and took 10,000 French prisoners. By night time, the preventing come to be taking location outside the trenches, inner French territory.

By February 25th, the French divisions who were defending Verdun a number of the town and the Meuse had suffered 60% casualties. And in this day, the French fort of Douaumont also fell.

Fort de Douaumont have become the most important citadel within the ring of nineteen shielding the city of Verdun. Built at some degree inside the past due 1800s, it became defended with gun turrets and had roof-reinforced concrete.

Unfortunately, in 1915 it changed into decided that the fortress (and the others within the protecting ring) became no longer probably to stand in competition to new German howitzer guns. Since it changed into within the once more of the enemy lines, the castle was stripped of most of its guns and provisions, and almost all its men, the ones being sent to areas wherein they were more crucial. Only 57 men remained.

When the Germans arrived, they just walked in via an undefended entrance— no pics had been fired.

The Germans superior to inside miles of Verdun, and there they stopped. The ground had thawed, and the land grow to be a bathroom; the infantry had no safety due to the fact the artillery couldn't get thru. To Falkenhayn, this changed into brilliant. They halted their enhance on February twenty ninth.

This grow to be particularly terrible to the morale of the French troops, and French Chief of Staff, Noel de Castlenau, wasn't having it. Verdun must be defended, so he brought in General Phillippe Pétain.

Pétain ordered the guys to stand their ground, and he set to work putting in location the French artillery to guard the street and ensuring that they'd a reliable deliver path. And that's what he did. Over the following week, 100 ninety,000 French troops had been transported to the the front along the "Sacred Way," a avenue strolling among Verdun and Bar-le-Duc. This avenue have become repaired and dedicated absolutely to vehicles and troops supporting the conflict, which moved 24 hours a day. Troops touring in this route had to walk in the fields; not something changed into allowed to block this road. Over 3,000 civilian and military automobiles had been used to transport munitions, and food—and to move divisions inner and out of the place.

After the initial wonder, the French rallied and from then, the Germans had their fingers whole. Pétain knew how trench battle labored. He favored confined offensives that most effective prolonged as a ways as his artillery may need to reach, and only after the enemy became battered, could probably his guys pass in.

By early March, the Germans changed their plan due to the reality they have been suffering heavier losses than that that they'd anticipated. Instead of taking the forts spherical Verdun, they decided to take any ground they will get, and try and ruin the French artillery. The French fought once more tough, and there has been an entire lot of movement earlier and backward for each facets. Hopes of a quick victory had been now dashed—via late March, the French had 89,000 casualties and the Germans, eighty,000.

Nobody should have enough money to go into reverse. By July, loads of masses of rounds have been fired and destruction changed into anywhere, corpses have been rotting inside the summer warmth, and flies made it even more depressing.

By the summer time, subjects have turn out to be even greater hard for the Germans. The Russians' Brusilov offensive had all started within the east, and the British and French had released the Battle of the Somme. The Germans had to skip troops far from Verdun, but the preventing nonetheless persisted for 6 extra months. The Germans came close sufficient to look the metropolis, but they in no manner captured it.

In September, strategist General Charles Mangin developed a plan to take again the out of place floor. In late October, the French prolonged-range weapons should batter the Germans for the duration of a wide vicinity, and a few days later, the infantry can also want to expand in the once more of a protect of artillery. By the midnight of the 24th, the French had regained Douaumont, together with 6,000 prisoners, and through November 2nd, the fortress at Vaux.

Next, Mangin envisage to push in advance to the genuine French traces, however because of terrible weather, their arrangements have been delayed and the Germans located of the plan. On December sixth they hit again, and the war continued for regular with week, which includes artillery and aircraft on each aspects. The French have been capable of push the Germans once more with the useful resource of way of December 18th, gaining eleven,000 greater prisoners and a hundred and fifteen guns in what changed into later referred to as the Battle of the Louvemont. This may be the surrender of the Battle of Verdun.

The Outcome

Verdun changed into one of the longest and bloodiest battles of the conflict, and it had a number one impact at the final effects. There were seven-hundred,000 casualties, with estimates that four hundred,000 had been French, and 3 hundred,000 German, which fell a protracted manner short of the German goal of bleeding the French navy dry. Consequently, German morale suffered notably, on the same time as the French were elated to had been able to shop Verdun and get higher the regions out of place in advance. But wellknown, there was now disillusionment and fatigue on all aspects of the struggle, which moved every person closer to the peace negotiations that would stand up in 1919 with the Treaty of Versailles.

This battle have come to be also very costly—the villages of Beaumont, Bezonvaux, Cumières, Douaumont, Fleury, Haumont, Louvemont, Ornes, and Vauxwere certainly destroyed. An vicinity of sixty five rectangular miles, called the "Red Zone" stays off-limits due to unexploded shells—together with a few with chemical payloads which can be simply as deadly in recent times as they were lower again then. Many of the useless have been buried through way of explosions and were in no way discovered. The stays that were located, each French and German, have been accumulated and are nowadays commemorated within the Douaumont Ossuary, which end up completed in 1923.

# Chapter 11: The Brusilov Offensive

Amajor Russian assault toward the Austro-Hungarian Empire led to big gains but also heavy casualties

In 1915–16, three meetings referred to as the Chantilly Conferences had been held maximum of the Allied powers—France, Britain, Russia, Serbia, and Italy—throughout which it turned into agreed that they may coordinate their forces to interrupt up and assault the Central Powers.

By 1916, as became going on in the west, the armies of the japanese the the front had been stuck in a stalemate of trench battle. Two years of war had added approximately little development.

In February 1916, the Germans have been attacking Verdun, and the French asked the Russians to attack Vilnius. It didn't circulate well—the Russians had five casualties for each one of the Germans. This strengthened the Germans' self guarantee, and that they had little fear of the Russians. One Austrian lieutenant colonel said, "They attack stupidly, in thick hundreds. They can do no greater because of the reality they haven't any schooling."

This end up a trustworthy assertion, given the Russian tendency to assault the use of a smooth brute force, human wave offensive fashion. This technique lacked method and nuance and changed into usually unsuccessful—specifically in the course of the extra current-day weapons of the time. The Russians had been additionally poorly geared up and definitely had little education.

The Russians have been discouraged, and their dreams began out to shift from an offensive stance to a protecting one. Aleksei Evert, the Imperial Army's Commander of the Western Front, desired to definitely dig in and protect the land they already had, in choice to go through any more losses.

But General Aleksei Brusilov, newly appointed General of the Southwestern Front, disagreed. He concept the

Russians were capable of plenty greater—they absolutely wanted higher weapons, training, and morale. Because the allies were all keeping the Central Powers occupied in terrific areas, he said it come to be a incredible time to release a primary strive within the east.

The plan become for Brusilov to attack inside the southwestern region, hoping to defeat as some of the Germans as possible as a diversion for Evert inside the north, who have to release his assault ten days after Brusilov inside the south. Evert should aim to triumph over the town of Vilnius, due to the fact the French had requested.

Brusilov moreover had a more sophisticated plan for the way the Russians might attack. Instead of transferring beforehand in massive groups (making smooth goals), he might unfold the men out to avoid having large numbers fall to artillery fireside. This manner, the Russians provided a far wider the front of assault, and after they have been in a position to interrupt thru enemy traces, reinforcements may additionally rush in to assist them.

Also, mastering from Russia's past errors, Brusilov's artillery can also carry out more strategic attacks, guided thru spotter planes who could help find out the high-quality locations to purpose, including areas wherein barbed twine or important trenches is probably destroyed. Brusilov moreover directed his guys to dig sap trenches to permit troops to get towards enemy traces in relative protection.

After an preliminary artillery bombardment, troops must attack in 4 waves. The first waves could encompass rifles and grenades. Next, the 0.33 wave might come through with system guns and make way for the fourth wave—the cavalry—who need to then pass thru the hollow.

All this changed into new to the Russians, so there was a period of giant education. Roles and duties were extra truely delineated, men acquired specific training the likes of which had in no way in advance than been supplied, and mock battles occurred.

The Russians have been feeling extra confident.

The Austro-Hungarians were feeling quite confident, as properly. They expected the Russians to stick to their playbook of in reality sending waves of fellows into gunfire. They had been in for a marvel.

The date became decided on: June 4, 1916, with the Battle of Lutsk.

The fight started out with artillery bombarding the trenches outdoor Lutsk. Spotter planes cited that 24 openings have been created in the defenses. Heavy artillery observed, however in preference to an prolonged barrage, the Russians made brief and strategic attacks towards strongholds at some point of the afternoon.

In the night time, as deliberate, assault troops moved out of the trenches, taking walks within the once more of the heavy artillery so their technique end up not obvious until they have been very close to the enemy strains.

The Russians were outnumbered, however they crushed the men inside the trenches. By the surrender of the day, they'd taken 26,000 prisoners. After in reality days, 130,000, and on June 7ththe Battle of Lutsk was over.

As Brusilov had hoped, the Austro-Hungarians had been forced to divert troops and guns from the the front in Italy. Counterattacks by means of way of Germany have been unsuccessful, and Germany had to divert property to the east, as properly.

To the south, the Russians made it as a protracted manner as the threshold of the Carpathian Mountains and captured the town of Chernivtsi, in which they have been in a role to threaten Hungary.

The Russians had been elated, and this huge push into enemy territory have become almost extraordinary at this thing in the war—plenty of the preventing up to now has been restrained to trenches. And no matter the truth that this offensive changed into only speculated to be a diversion to attract interest away from the north, the Russians had been now in a function to win a big victory.

At the appointed time, Evert grow to be to assault inside the north using the equal strategies that had been so a achievement for Brusilov. Instead, he despatched phrase that there could be a do away with. He stated his troops had been inadequately knowledgeable, and now not prepared to stand struggle. He stated the climate turned into stopping them, and that the German defenses were too sturdy.

Evert stalled till July 3rd, costing the Russians the benefit of wonder.

Czar Nicholas II determined on a trade of plan: Brusilov's offensive ought to now be the primary motive. He despatched men and gadget to the south.

Brusilov become livid, however he had no time for that. He speedy made a brand new plan to push earlier to the metropolis of Kovel after which north to Baranavichy, wherein there were railroads the Russians may want to use to transport similarly west to Lviv.

However, due to the delays, German reinforcements arrived. The Germans were more difficult to conquer than the

Austro-Hungarians, and the Russians discovered themselves dropping floor.

Finally, Evert come to be ready to assault inside the north. Unfortunately, in location of schooling his guys using Brusilov's strategies, he had determined to apply the conventional Russian tactic of simply pointing his troops at the enemy and having them stroll inside the course of the guns. He out of place one hundred,000 men and won almost not anything in go back.

Brusilov have emerge as going for walks out of educated troops, and the reinforcements who have been arriving did now not have the capabilities to take Kovel. The Germans hit lower returned, and the Russians must nice dig in and set up a present day-day the front line. They made no similarly advances.

By the give up of September, the offensive became over.

The Outcome

The Brusilov Offensive had a protracted manner-attaining and giant consequences at the conflict. First, even though it did now not cross completely according to plot, it turn out to be Russia's biggest and maximum successful advertising campaign of the conflict. It decimated Austria-Hungary, and then element, they were now not effective inside the warfare and in no way absolutely recovered. In the stop, Germany took over their ultimate troops.

The Central Powers had half of of a million casualties, and Russia is stated to have suffered greater than a million. Many of these blanketed expert soldiers who have been now not without problems modified.This should lessen Russia's capability to keep to fight.

The Brusilov Offensive moreover drew desired guys far from special battles, achieving its motive of relieving strain on the Allies at Verdun and the Somme.

If Evert had cooperated, subjects may additionally have labored out better. But because it stood, possibly the maximum critical impact of the Brusilov Offensive have come to be lower again in Russia. Here, the incompetent manage and shortage of existence are stated to have brought about the

Russian Revolution and the withdrawal of Russia from the warfare in Europe.

Brusilov went right away to assist shape the Red Army.

The Battle of Tannenberg

A primary German victory over the Russian military marked the start of the surrender of Russian involvement inside the battle

When battle broke out in August 1914, each the Germans and the Russians knew it have become coming. In the wake of the assassination of Archduke Franz Ferdinand, Germany may combat in protection of the Austro-Hungarian Empire, and the Russians on behalf of their fine friend, Serbia. The Battle of Tannenberg have become one of the earliest battles of the war, and its very last effects may additionally want to set the tone for the war that accompanied.

Early in 1914, in his discussions with the British and French, General Yakov Grigoryevich Zhilinsky agreed that the Russians ought to offer 800,000 troops within 15 days of mobilization, and also that they may interact in a plan to assault the Germans.

Two Russian armies had been mobilized underneath Generals Paul von Rennenkampf and Alexander Samsonov. Rennenkampf modified into to assault East Prussia and draw the Germans there, and days later, Samsonov became to move into Germany to the south in a bid to encircle the Germans and push them far from the Vistula River.

One trouble with this plan grow to be that the Russians themselves had destroyed infrastructure like roads and railways close to the border in an attempt to prevent German improve there. Consequently, while Rennenkamf made his flow into inside the north, Samsonov's troops had been coping with transport and deliver troubles inside the south, leaving them worn-out, under-prepared, and usually disorganized.

On the western the front, the Germans were engaged inside the Schlieffen Plan, in which they was hoping to short knock France out of the warfare and then flip their full interest to the Russians. It have turn out to be their expectation that the Russians wouldn't be able to mobilize troops fast enough to be a problem so early inside the struggle.

In fact, the Russians were now not nicely organized for this initiative. Slowed through a lack of infrastructure and bad company, they might war to even arrive on the the the front, relying on horses and an underdeveloped railway device to move guys at some stage in the huge and rugged expanse of the u . S . Toward the japanese border. Furthermore, their communications code changed into speedy deciphered thru the Germans and despite the fact that they did create a brand new one, most of the commanders didn't have the brand new code e-book, so they as an opportunity broadcast sensitive data without any obvious try and hide it.

## The Battle

As 500,000 Russian soldiers moved east into Germany, the 2 armies have become separated thru the large device of the Masurian lakes. Zhilinski pressured the beleaguered Samsonov to transport speedy, believing that the Germans may be pressured to retreat at the back of the Vistula.

Had it been as plenty as German General Max von Prittwitz, this could surely have occurred. On August 20th, on the same time as Samsonov's army turn out to be stated to be advancing on the southern fringe of East Prussia, he called a assembly with of his group of workers, General Paul Grünert, and Lieutenant Colonel Max Hoffmann, further to his leader of employees, General Georg Friedrich Wilhelm, Graf von Waldersee. Anxious that the approaching Russians may additionally want to circle within the again of the German forces and reduce off his line of retreat, Prittwitz knowledgeable the alternative guys that they may bypass over again within the lower again of the Vistula to save you such an occurrence. The special guys disagreed, however Prittwitz knowledgeable them that it became his desire to make, and he left the room.

In his absence, Grünert and Hoffman satisfied Waldersee that this have turn out to be a horrible concept, but none of them might be conscious that Prittwitz had lengthy gone to make a few calls. He had added his plans to retreat, and consequently, his opportunity, Paul von Hindenburg, collectively along with his chief of personnel, Erich von Ludendorff, had been on their way. The awesome guys may not find out this improvement for two days at the equal time as Prittwitz's elimination have become obvious.

In taking on the German Eighth Army, Ludendorff's plan changed into aligned with Hoffman's—he wanted to transport in opposition to Samsonov's left flank, however the Germans had too few men to be powerful. Eyeing Rennenkampf making little development westward in the north, Ludendorff determined to threat moving the majority of the German troops to the south.

Here, they took gain of the Russians' terrible communication and lack of visibility. Under Ludendorff, General Hermann von Francois turn out to be tasked with attacking the Russian left wing, at which factor the Russian flank withdrew. Francois pursued them and determined on August 28th that that they had retreated an extended way sufficient that he might also need to get spherical and within the again of the center column of the Russian forces, which he did.

If Samsonov had appeared what emerge as taking region within the flanks of his military, he might have had more time to invite for help from Rennenkampf. He can also have despatched guys from the center to his flanks or perhaps retreated. As it have emerge as, by the point he observed out that his hungry and demoralized guys were virtually surrounded and surrendering through way of the thousands, it became too late. He went into the woodland and ended his personal life in location of face the final effects.

## The Outcome

The Battle of Tannenberg, named for the village near the middle of the motion, in present day-day Poland, turn out to be a clean victory for the Germans and had the effect of halting the Russian grow to be Prussia. After their fulfillment, Hindenburg and Ludendorff were taken into consideration heroes and might be primary figures in some unspecified time in the future of the rest of the warfare. (It should perhaps be mentioned that the actual architect of the technique grow to be Hoffman, and General Francois finished a notable element as nicely, but they didn't get lots credit.) The recognition of the German military in widespread become increased, as became morale. The Germans took 90 ,000 prisoners, in addition to sources, ammunition, and a large kind of guns—over four hundred pieces of artillery.

The Germans suffered 13,000 casualties, while the Russians had 30,000 killed or wounded guys.

For their element, defeat on this struggle end up a sour tablet for the Russians. They need to scarcely have enough money the losses of fellows and weaponry—and furthermore, the defeat highlighted the folly and incompetence of broadcasting un-coded radio communications. Lastly, after Samsonov's defeat, the Germans had been able to refresh their forces and pass at once to defeat Rennenkampf, as nicely, resulting in even extra losses of fellows and system.

## Chapter 12: The Middle East

Just as World War I left its scars in Europe, it modified into a time of violence, strife, and transformation inside the Middle East, as well. The conflict here became shaped with the aid of the competing pastimes of severa worldwide powers which include the British Empire, Russia, the Ottoman Empire, and the Arab countries.

We'll speak some of the number one conflicts: the Gallipoli Campaign, the Siege of Kut, and the Arab Revolt.

The Gallipoli Campaign

## The Campaign

Turkey, having been in decline for two centuries, did no longer right away be part of the conflict at its outbreak, although each the Entente and the Central Powers preferred the empire to enroll in on their aspect. But Turkey had a hard relationship with Russia and became getting a few resource from Germany, so whilst the British interfered in the acquisition of two naval ships the Ottomans have been seeking out, the Turks sided with the Central Powers.

On October 27th, 1914, a number of Russian ports at the Black Sea were attacked via warships underneath the Ottoman flag. This compelled Russia to transport troops and assets from its western the the front to the Caucasus region, and Britain and France now needed to discover a manner to help them. They devised a way to advantage a foothold inside the Gallipoli Peninsula. From proper right here, they was hoping to defeat the Turks and benefit a right away route to Russia via the Black Sea.

With fifteen divisions at their disposal, together with British troops from India, Australia, and New Zealand, further to 3 Russian and French troops from the Orient, the British predicted they'll need 50,000 to 70,000 guys. The Greeks advised they could need 3 instances that quantity, but had been not noted, the Allies being confident that the Turks should now not present a notable impediment to their navy might also.

Under General Sir Ian Hamilton, forces have been assembled in Egypt. His plan turn out to be to advantage access to the peninsula so the Allied forces have to control the Dardanelle Straits, permitting get right of entry to for naval ships to pass thru to Constantinople.

On the Ottoman side, the Fifth Army have turn out to be commanded via the use of German General Liman von Sanders, who aimed to maintain control of the high ground along the peninsula to save you the Allied forces from passing with the resource of land or with the resource of using sea.

On March 18th, 1915, the Allied fleet (which includes their oldest warships, due to the truth the Ottoman Navy wasn't nicely appointed) sailed to the Dardanelles. Overconfident, they sailed too near the shore and were attacked through the Turks' shore defenses. They withdrew, but no longer in advance than dropping    British battleships and suffering harm to a third. The French moreover out of region one supply and its group of six hundred guys.

On April twenty fifth, Allied floor forces landed in  places on the west side of the peninsula. Due to a navigation errors, a few Australian and New Zealander troops ended up hundreds farther north than predicted, in what's now called ANZAC Cove (Australian and New Zealand Army Corps).Because the attack modified into no longer predicted, the Ottoman forces did not have enough men to defeat them— however the hard terrain and their feature at the immoderate floor had been useful and 2000 of the Allied troops had been killed. The remainder dug in close to the shore.

Over the subsequent 8 months, the ones guys may also bear the extreme warm temperature of summer season and the cold of wintry climate, and overcrowding in terrible situations— together with the presence of unburied corpses and their attendant, incessant flies—ought to necessarily lead to outbreaks of typhoid and dysentery. There became little food and water, and the lice-ridden guys had been packed in deep trenches on a small vicinity of coastline with little or no shade or refuge. Because of the Turks at the floor above them, getting access to hospital therapy and factors from the ships changed into very tough.

The other landing befell on five beaches, which have been precise S, V, W, X, and Y. In all positions, the touchdown forces met with resistance from the Turks, and because of a lack of orders, dug in close to the shore—which ultimately added about heavy casualties on each elements, and an eventual stalemate.

The invading forces had to take the immoderate ground, however they have been now not capable of dislodge the Turks. The Turks had been relying on their artillery to repel the Allies however had been venture to supporting fireside from the ships. Soon, Turkish reinforcements arrived, and via May and June, the opposing forces everywhere in the peninsula driven backward and forward, with heavy casualties on every elements, but no profits. The very last engagement took place on June third.

Hamilton requested for additonal men, but the Allies had been distracted because of the fact Bulgaria had joined the warfare on the factor of the Central Powers. The request modified into refused, and in October, Hamilton changed into changed thru Lieutenant-General Sir Charles Monro. The selection to withdraw from the peninsula changed into made. Almost all the men had been moved out by way of manner of the surrender of the 12 months, and the advertising and advertising and marketing campaign officially resulted in January.

The Outcome

It have grow to be a brief but bloody marketing marketing campaign that become a failure for the Allies because of a loss of planning, hard terrain, illness, and strong resistance from the Turks. British First Lord of the Admiralty, Winston Churchill, would possibly surrender. In all, it's anticipated that 500,000 Allied troops participated, and 315,000were at the Ottoman side. Reports vary, however it's expected that the Allied forces suffered 189,000 killed and wounded, whilst the Turks had 162,000.

The failure of this advertising marketing campaign turn out to be however some other blow to Russia, dashing their hopes of gaining resources and useful resource from the Black Sea. It can be each other contributing hassle in their eventual decline.

Anzac Day, (April twenty fifth) remains found in Australia and New Zealand to honor the squaddies who served there.

The Siege of Kut

The Siege of Kut modified proper right into a horrible failure for the British navy, wherein nearly 15,000 guys were hemmed in on the metropolis of Kut from December seventh, 1915, until April twenty ninth, 1916.

The number one goal for British forces in Mesopotamia was to defend their oil pursuits, which have become completed via securing the town of Basra, in cutting-edge-day Iraq. However, the British commanders have been seduced through the usage of visions of marching into Baghdad.

In 1915, the British Army were often advancing up the Tigris River within the path of Baghdad, but now the sixth Division of the Indian Army beneath Charles Townshend turned into falling back after a a fulfillment however luxurious engagement at Ctesiphon. There have been many unwell and wounded (4,500 from both components of the battle) and not enough to resist any greater attacks from the Ottomans, no longer to mention going ahead to Baghdad. The journey backtrack the Tigris River become miserable—lengthy and without appropriate sufficient medical additives.

When they arrived at Kut, Townshend and his advanced, General John Nixon, determined they would take a stand there. Townshend claimed his guys had been exhausted and will flow no further, and it modified right into a defensible feature in the curve of the river, and Nixon preferred to tie up the Ottoman forces. Now the metropolis, whose real populace changed into about 6,500, now moreover supported 14,500 British and Indian troops, citizens, and 2,000 ill and wounded. Townshend at once ordered remedy, however he did not immediately restriction his men's rations.

Townsend changed right into a useless and ambitious guy who desired to be seen as a hero. There are some doubts about his management on this rely wide variety—some declare he have to have made it once more to Basra and prevented a siege, however he craved the attention and the danger to be promoted.

On December 7th, they were surrounded with the aid of using manner of a pressure of eleven,000 Turk infantrymen commanded thru Khalil Pasha and Baron von der Goltz— an professional German desired who had spent years with the Ottoman navy. These forces attacked the British in Kut 3 instances inside the direction of December, and then issue Goltz ordered the development of siege fortifications and despatched men down the river to dam off the deliver route.

After a gradual response because of bureaucratic deliberations over how many guys to ship, the primary comfort excursion approached in January 1916, which induced the Battle of Sheikh Sa'ad. Troops underneath Major-General George Younghusband and Lieutenant-General Sir Fenton John Aylmer approached Kut along every sides of the river, with Younghusband's guys on the left, and the forces on the proper commanded with the aid of Major-General Sir George Kemball. On the eighth and 9th of January, they pushed in advance, and the Turks retreated 10 miles to Wadi, a river valley on a tributary of the Tigris, in which they took up positions on every elements of the river.

On January thirteenth, Aylmer attacked the left financial group, pushing the

Ottomans lower back some other 5 miles to Hanna, in which they suffered 2,seven-hundred killed and wounded. On January 19th, General Nixon modified into changed through the usage of Lieutenant-General Sir Percy Lake. Aylmer acquired more guys, and on March eighth, he attacked at Dujaila redoubt, wherein he out of region four,000 of them. He have grow to be modified with the useful useful resource of General George Gorringe.

At this issue, Khalil Pasha arrived with over 20,000 reinforcements.

In the metropolis, the guys had withstood the cold and torrential rain, and food was taking walks out. The British men had been able to consume the draught animals: oxen, horses, or even camels, however the Indian troops had been in massive part vegetarian. Many of those held out till they had been all of the way right down to only some oz. Of grain in step with day; others had been pressured to eat meat if you need to stay on.

For the primary time in records, airplanes dropped materials—but their success became confined. The German planes avoided maximum of the supply planes from getting through, and loads of drops went into the river, or maybe into territory controlled thru way of the Turks. Those received were not nearly enough to prevent hunger.

Finally, on April fifth, Gorringe arrived with approximately 30,000 troops. They had some preliminary successes at Fallahiya and Bait Isa, but after they reached Sannaiyat on April 22nd, they were no longer able to pass. This may be the forestall of the comfort attempt.

After 30,000 Allied squad dies were killed or wounded in an attempt to break the Siege of Kut, it became time to surrender. In a final-ditch strive, Townshend proposed a ransom to allow his guys to go unfastened—£2 million—which is probably £167 million these days. The Turks, confident after their achievement at Gallipoli, refused the payout.

The ceasefire come to be installation on April twenty 6th, and after 147 days, Townshend surrendered at the 29th of April, 1916.

Surrender

When Townsend sooner or later capitulated, having secured an assure from Pasha that his canine, Spot, might be dispatched appropriately once more to England, Townshend have become sent upriver to Baghdad in which he waited out the relaxation of the conflict in comfort, being treated as an crucial traveler and taken to severa cultural websites within the place. Most of his officials had been additionally properly cared for.

There were over thirteen, 000 guys who did not fare so properly—Indian officers and Indian and British soldiers, which includes the wounded. About 1,3 hundred sick and wounded guys have been allowed to move away, together with seven-hundred or for you to generally tend them. The enlisted guys—all of whom had already continued starvation and the difficult instances of the siege—were then forced on a demise march inside the barren location warmth and dirt without water, meals, or clinical hobby, all of the while being harassed and beaten via manner of their Ottoman guards. The useless have been left wherein they fell. Those who survived the journey decided no consolation, because the conditions in the camps had been simply as horrible. Here, a few had been located to artwork at the railroads, and lots of died of cholera, dysentery, and enteritis. At the quit of the warfare, most effective 30% of the British who have been taken have been despite the fact that alive. The four, 000 Muslim Indian soldiers have been handled better, and masses of them joined the Turks.

The Outcome

The Siege of Kut changed into one of the most sizeable screw ups of the British navy. The repeated disasters of the comfort forces to free the town, the starvation and absence of lifestyles of the guys, and the eventual give up are all a delivery of humiliation. And it end up for nothing: ten months later, the British had taken the entire region.

The Turks left Kut in February 1917, and Baghdad fell to the British in March. In the aftermath of the battle, there has been an inquiry as to why Townshend come to be ordered to march north to Baghdad in any respect considering British oil pastimes had been already served thru the acquisition of Basra. Many guys had been positioned to be partly guilty, but Townshend has turned out to be no longer amongst them. In reality, he has become knighted.

Still, whilst the warfare had ended and the tale of the surrender at Kut changed into instructed, Townshend's days of comfort close to Constantinople were seen in evaluation to the situations his guys persisted, and the humans heard in their countless, horrible deaths. Perhaps the maximum crucial lesson of the Siege of Kut is the terrible rate men pays on the equal time because the leaders of battle are more interested by glory than their welfare.

www.ingramcontent.com/pod-product-compliance
Lightning Source LLC
Chambersburg PA
CBHW071342120626
46546CB00002B/657